HEY MA,
IT'S THE DOGGY MAN!

BARRY MCDONOUGH

Dedication

To Mum and Dear Auntie Ronnie,
also Gemma, Grace, and Jessica.

Table of Contents

Acknowledgements

The author would sincerely love to thank the people who sponsored him to ensure this book got published. They include Fairyhouse Market, Alverno House Laytown, The Cottage Inn Laytown, Patt Boshell Laytown, Robert Watson Laytown, Lynch's Caravan Park Bettystown, The Neptune Hotel Bettystown, Hyland and Boland Estate Agents Bettystown, Pilltown Driving Range, Doneycarney Football Club, Rocco Macari Food Chain, John Ryan Estate Agent Ashbourne, N2 Electric Ashbourne, The Travel Shop Ashbourne, Denis Fox Publican Ashbourne, Tighe Riordan Motors Ashbourne, Molly's Bar Ashbourne, Coolquay Lodge Coolquay, Scotch Hall Jewellers Drogheda, Lime Kiln Gastro Pub and shop Julianstown, Paul Kelly's Vet and Animal Hospital Ratoath.

Also Master Clinton Bates and Sir Jacky Hanon.

The Author would like to thank "Koka Lime Design Ltd" for the images and illustrations that they provided. Vinny Hearns for all the support and help in transcribing the book to a digital format. To the Editor of the book Caroline Feeney, I am deeply grateful for her tireless work and help in the construction on this book. Choice Publishing for their help, knowledge and guidance through the whole process, I offer my sincere thanks.

Finally, I would like to thank the wonderful staff at the Iberostar Founty Beach Agadir, Morocco for their marvellous help during the time that I was writing this book.

Foreword

Many of my friends have said to me that I should write a book about my life, but I don't like memoirs or autobiographies. Why? Because they are usually written by people who "boast about themselves or their achievements."

That is not the case when it comes to Barry McDonough. Barry has a story to tell, he condenses three score years of living into a humorous, sometimes hilarious and entertaining narrative of his life with dogs over a period of sixteen years. His relationship with the canine species is one of love, fun and respect. He loves dogs; dogs of every breed, size and variety. He has collected dogs from their owners and brought them to *"Le Paws Dog Grooming Salon"* and after washing, grooming and dare I say spoiling by Colette, he brings them back to their homes looking gorgeous and beautiful to the delight of their owners. It is obvious from his writings that dogs have developed a liaison with Barry in response to his gentle, considerate caring nature and understanding of their temperament and individual character.

This autobiographical reminiscence also gives us a glimpse of family life in a Co Meath sea-side town in the 1960's, highlighting the excitement of summers with the influx of thousands of day trippers contrasting with the desolation of winters when his mother would shut down the family business, and her extended family entertained themselves with singing, dancing and recitations.

Barry and his lovely partner Collette are inveterate travellers having visited such far flung places as, South Africa, United States, Egypt, Morocco, Turkey to mention a few. All of their trips are related as tales of fun and enjoyment and of meeting simple peasants in desert settings in North Africa meeting Hollywood starts in theatres and nightclubs of Los Angeles and Las Vegas.

Vince Hearns
A fellow holiday maker.

Preface

Having spent thirty years farming in Bettystown, working 365 days a year with no let up, from midnight calving, twice-a-day milking of 50 cows to the constant cleaning, worrying etc involved, it was time for a change. So just like that I up and moved to Ashbourne with my partner Collette who had just finished an intensive Dog Grooming course in Belfast and "le Paws" was born. To help get Collette started I was drafted in to drop and collect the dogs for her to groom. Sixteen years later and I'm still doing it.

Some of the characters I have met and situations I have found myself in over the years absolutely beggar belief, so I felt I had to get them down on paper. The one phrase over the years that will haunt me forever comes from one young member of a household when I arrived at 07:30am to collect her dog for grooming. "Ma, It's the doggy man," she shouted as she opened the door - hence the book title.

As I stated earlier I farmed for over thirty years and I still loves cows but Dogs are my life now. While farming had its good points at times, I'm afraid the dogs will always be my first choice. The look of a well-groomed dog happily smiling is a sight to behold. The grateful owners, happy to see their fur babies arrive home - clean gorgeous and smelling like a Dolce and Gabbana model gives pleasure to all.

The stories in this book have made my life with dogs hilarious and joyful. I have laughed uncontrollably at some of the situations I have met and I hope you will too.

Chapter 1
Getting started

McDonough's Fancy Goods was my mother's shop in Laytown, the small seaside village where I was brought up. Mam sold everything that was not fancy - sweets, drinks and clothes which would find their way into a vintage collection even now. We also sold daily papers which I had to deliver to all the locals on weekends. It was right next to the Railway station where in the summer months, half of Dublin descended on us for a swim and an ice cream. Up the road about half a mile was Butlin's holiday camp and people from the North of Ireland and Dublin used to flock to Laytown because of its close proximity to the station.

During the winter it was desolate. Mum loved the winter because she could gossip with the locals who came in and because she could give them the attention she reckoned they deserved but didn't get during the busy summers. My best memories of childhood were Laytown in the winter. Mum closed the shop and would have us performing for her in our old Kitchen. My older brothers were too cool to perform, and my sisters were shy. Me, I sang like a lark until my voice annoyed her.

My Mam loved those shows - she loved to see us showing our artistic sides. Every time my cousins came over from London we would have a show in the Garage out the back. Anne, my older cousin was in charge of Production. She organised a big curtain so that we were as professional as possible. I would often open the show with a song – normally a Sean Dunphy hit called *"If I could choose."* George, my cousin did impressions of Wilfred Barrell from *"Til death us part"* and we sometimes had ad-lib from Jenny and Brian. And then we would finish off with a rousing Chorus from *"The Sound of Music."* Mam, Auntie Ronnie and my dear Auntie Nellie would give us a rousing reception and then the curtain would finally fall on us. To this day I can remember all this, and might I add the curtain may have fallen on us but it never came down on us!

My friends were all there. Jerry, whose father was a station master, Brian whose dad was the local butcher and Pat and Jimmy whose father was a gentleman farmer. Brian had red hair, so we named him Lennie, Pat was the oldest so no name for him, Jimmy was Pat's younger brother, so we called him toddler. I had big rosy cheeks, so they called me Rosy and Jerry was known as JJ. To this day I still have great contact with Brian, Lennie, and JJ.

On Bank holiday weekends hundreds of bikers used to come into Laytown, park up and create havoc. Well, not really havoc, just having fun. Loud music and bottles of beer in public. My dad would go mad, calling them tramps and layabouts, mam never did though. Deep down I think she admired the fun they were having, having said that she always loved Marlon Brando in *"The Wild One's."* Later mam sold the shop and we moved to Bettystown but Bettystown was not for me. I refused to move and my dad said, "Leave him there, he will soon learn," but I did not. Two and a half weeks I stayed on my own. Everyone knew I was there, and everyday food was brought to me with the promise "Don't tell your dad." It was heaven to know that at fourteen I could survive on my own. After a month, the shop was sold and off to Bettystown I went with a broken heart. Twenty-three years I spent in Bettystown, worked a farm that made my dad a million, worked a bar that made my uncle a fortune. I was never short of money, but I was never happy. That is not until I found the perfect woman and the perfect job for a man who loves animals the way I do.

Chapter 2
How our family grew

Our love of dogs was evident from the start. We had Lizzie a cantankerous Shih tzu who needed company and no better company could she have had than Dino, who was in a Drogheda pet shop and as we passed he jumped up the side of his cage and demanded to be brought home. So we did. A magnificent looking Shih Tzu, cocky, confident, and full of himself, Dino was family straight away. Lizzie was getting on in years however and we reckoned that Dino needed some fun in his life, so Frankie joined us from Trim.

We went to view him on a Saturday afternoon in the summer. One of a beautiful litter of five pups he crawled over to Collette and melted her heart. Welcome Frankie! Another beautiful Shih Tzu and always happy, we quickly formed a relationship with Dino that would last forever. Enter Freddie.

Six months and many dropped hints later, Toy Poodle Freddie jumped out of a roses tin and straight into a surprised Collette's arms. Freddie was a game changer. Small but huge in personality he was christened Freddie after Freddie Mercury. He behaved just like the great Queen frontman, strutting around the house as if he owned it. And of course Freddie had to have a companion too and the most beautiful Toy Poodle of them all arrived 2 months later. Lucy, elegant, stylish with a loving way about her that matched her stunning looks. Lulu, another beautiful Top Poodle we rescued joined us soon thereafter and she was followed by two Black Poodle beauties, Beauty and Simone. Our ménage of dogs was complete or so you would have thought but No, one final piece of the jigsaw was needed and that was Mika, the most gorgeous creature on God's earth. Light Brown in colour with a beautiful face she was just an overall stunning Chihuahua.

If Freddie was the king, then Mika was the Queen. Not for her too much of the outdoor life! A small visit outside during which her subjects gathered around her and then she would return to her throne, high above everyone else. Mika would watch the daily goings on, surveying everything with her royal gaze and growling menacingly if upset in any way. No question about it, Mika was the Lady of the House.

We had started to frequent Fairyhouse Market every Sunday at this time, and we eventually decided to start selling in it. Collette had been offered the chance of a course in Belfast but it was expensive so we put our heads together and we figured we could cover the cost by doing this and it did work out well. We did the Market on Sunday, Collette would go to Belfast on the Monday morning and return on Thursday, tough going at times but we got there – the girl who cut hair on Humans was about to hit the canine world! Fairyhouse market helped us a lot back then and I'm still there to this day.

Six months later Colette was fully qualified, and we had lift off. It was 2007, there was a recession, we had no money and no jobs- not the best year to start a business but from the beginning we thrived. People love their dogs like they love their children and we just got busier and busier. I wasn't supposed to be part of the business, but we had decided we would drop and collect for the first few weeks to get things going. Sixteen years later I am still doing it and I would not have it any other way.

Chapter 3
Bobby the springer spaniel

On a bright September morning I was heading to Rathfeigh about ten miles outside Ashbourne and a short hop from our grooming salon in Ashbourne to collect Bobby a springer spaniel, when it occurred to me - Crikey I forgot to write down the address!

Still not to worry I thought, Rathfeigh is so small I will have no problem plus I had the owners name Mark McEntee. I called into a service station in Rathfeigh for a paper and casually asked if they knew of a Mark who had a springer Spaniel and where he lived. "Yes" says the girl behind the counter. "He lives on the upper Road," telling me that he would be out walking Bobby now and I would see him on the road. I drove out onto the road and happily for me spotted Mark and his Springer Spaniel Bobby just a minute later. I pulled up and greeted him with a hearty "Good Morning."

"And a very good Morning to you," replied Mark. "God Mark," I said, "he looks in fine fettle." "Ah Yes," he replied. "He's on the best of Grub and I walk him three times a day. Sometimes past the post office and sometimes up to the new estate they have just built, but always three times a day." "Does he hunt?" I asked Mark. "No," he replied. "He used to, but the Do-gooders are trying to stop all that sort of thing now. So I just give him plenty of exercise to make it up."

"Right," I said and jumped out of the van. "Well let's get him trimmed up and cleaned."

Sometimes a dog can be wary of you and back away, but not Bobby – no he jumped happily into my arms and gave me a big kiss and smiled happily out of the cage I had just put him in. "Anything special?" I asked Mark regarding Bobby. "No," says Mark. "Nothing at all."

I jumped back into the van and rolled down the window and said, "I should be back about flourish, is that good with you?" "Yes," says Mark "that should be good." I was about to pull off when Mark knocked on the window. "Excuse me," he said "But who are you?" "Who am I?" says I. "We are Le Paws, the dog groomers. I am bringing your dog for grooming." "Oh very good," says Mark.

"Yeah" We spoke to you on Monday, and you booked Bobby in, Remember?" "No," says Mark "I don't have a phone." I stuttered out, "but you booked him in with Collette. I have you here – Mark McEntee." "Ahh. No my name is Mark McAuley. Mark McEntee lives on the upper road further up. A lovely man he is, but still mourning his Dad who passed away 2 months ago. He is still not over it but he will in time. He has a dog too." I stumbled out of the van.

"Yes," Mark says. "A lovely King Charles. He got him in Tralee last summer. A lovely little animal"

Embarrassed as hell I dragged myself to the back of the van and released Bobby from his cell. None the worse for wear, Bobby once again jumped into my arms and gave me a final kiss before bouncing back to his owner. I jumped back into the van and mumbled an apology for my mistake to Mark. Not in the slightest bit perturbed,

Mark waved cheerily and told me to enjoy the rest of my day. As I went to drive off, I stopped, rolled down the window and said to Mark, "I have just stopped you on the road, taken your dog and put him into the back of a van of someone you do not know. I was on the point of driving off. Did it not occur to you to ask me anything?" "No," says Mark "Not at all. You seemed to know what you were doing. Bye now."

I drove away totally bemused. Someday I said I would write a book. I would love to know what Bobby would have said.

Chapter 4

Dogs have feelings too

Anyone who thinks that dogs are just emotionless pets should have met the lovely Lucy, a German shepherd who came to us every fortnight for a wash and brush for two years. To explain fully, Lucy had a constant companion all her life - a beautiful Lab cross called Molly who unfortunately died. Devoted owners Brian decided what with both of them working long hours, Lucy needed a day out every two weeks – something for her to look forward to. And she sure as hell did! From the moment I picked her up at 7am in the morning, until she went home that evening she lapped up every minute of it. Lucy used to look at me the way young girls looked at Donny Osmond and David Cassidy - complete devotion.

She was a wonderfully gentle and compliant soul with not a bad bone or bark in her - well that was until one day when I picked up Lucy early as usual and she was washed, brushed dried and went for her normal afternoon snooze while listening to Today FM. That same afternoon, we got a call to see if we could fit in a young Labrador with a lovely nature called Sonya who happened to have escaped that morning and visited her local ditch. Covered from top to tail in filth, this lovely young cream Labrador arrived looking almost Brown! Straight into the bath with her, Collette foamed and scrubbed and had her gleaming within an hour. Sonya's owner had asked if we could be as quick as possible as she had a kid's party on, and the kids loved Sonya to be there.

"Maybe you could hand dry her with the blaster," suggested Collette as the lady was under a little pressure to get her home.

With that I brought her to the back of the salon, where Lucy was snoozing and proceeded to hand dry Sonya. Like all Labradors Sonya revelled in this personal attention and stood quietly smiling happily. I glanced towards Lucy who was not sleeping any more. Ears pricked and eyes blazing she emerged from the cage which I never closed and started to push Sonya away with her head. Having done that she stood there taking away all the heat although fully dry. Amid a fit of giggles Collette moved Sonya into the cage and thought that would placate Lucy. Not a bit of it! Lucy nosed open the cage door and fixed Sonya with a steely glare – "out" was the message.

Sonya got out and scuttled into an adjoining cage. Drier off, Lucy ambled back to her own spot and commenced her sleeping posture, but with one eye open, basically letting Sonya know "you may be younger, and you may be gorgeous, but this Tramp (me) is still going my way!"

On another occasion, Kim rang me from Wexford one morning where Lucy was with them on holidays in their mobile home by the sea. "Barry" she said, "can you do Lucy tomorrow." "Sure Kim," I said, "but I assumed you were down there for the week." "We are" said Kim "but someone has Today FM on, and Lucy keeps looking to see where you are so Brian is going to bring her up this evening and back down tomorrow."

Devoted owners and devoted dogs can really make this a rewarding Business!

Lucy, Devoted

Chapter 5
Do you ever get bitten?

Do you ever get bitten? is a question I am constantly asked. Rarely is always the answer, but with one exception - an early morning collection in Bettystown for a new customer, a medium sized collie cross or so we were informed. I arrived bang on time and the owner went out the back to bring in Lucifer.

"Come on Darling," I heard her shout, then in came Lucifer. A giant half Doberman half Devil, god he was well named. Lucifer fixed me with a steady stare, as if to say, "And you are?" Out to the van and with a lot of coaxing from his owner, Lucifer reluctantly went into cage. I set off for the salon but was brought to an abrupt stop by an agonised howl from the back. I stopped to check him, opened the door and there was Lucifer, who had eaten his way out of the holding cage, eyeballing me with intent. He saw a chance and he bolted for freedom, but I managed to get a hand on him and put him back. He lunged again and once again I managed to repel him, only this time he managed to snare half my hand in his mouth. Pain shot through me, but the fear of him bolting into the wilderness was a worse pain.

I managed to get my hand from between his molar's and got the door shut. Straight back to his home, hand bleeding profusely, I knocked at his owner's door. "Sorry," I said, "but Lucifer won't be groomed with us," as I would not be putting Collette's life in danger. "Why?" she asked, and I showed her my hand, which at this stage resembled a scene from nightmare on elm street. "Oh" she replied, "that's so unlike him," she said, "he must not be in the best of humour." "Can I have something to stop the bleeding?" I asked. "Oh I have some kitchen towel here, I will bring it to you, as I've just washed the floor." Hand bandaged in kitchen towel; I took off for home but within a minute there was blood all over the van floor. Luckily my doctor, Joe Gremin is in Bettystown, so I pulled up outside and raced for the front door. There were about five people of advancing years inside, when I came crashing through the door with a trail of blood in my wake. The look of horror on their faces as I strode in was not good. Luckily, Joe was at reception at the time and hauled me in straight away. Three stitches in my hand, a wad of bandages and a tetanus shot for good measure. Back to Ashbourne thirty minutes later and into the salon, throbbing hand like a glove puppet and still rattling. I was met by Collette who casually asked, "Well, anything new?" "Other than a few stitches not a lot new," I retorted.

Chapter 6

Buster from Ballymun and other dogs

"Hi Barry, could you pick buster up in the morning?" "Yes Janice," says I. "I'll be there about seven." "Ah Barry," was the reply "I will still have me curlers in. I'll leave the key, let yourself in, see you in the afternoon." For eight years I picked up buster from Ballymun early in the morning and returned him back at lunchtime. Phone contact only, I never even met her until one day in Charlestown shopping centre, she came up to me and said, "Ah Barry how are you!" I had not a clue who she was. "It's Janice from Ballymun," she shouted "Buster." "Sorry Janice" I replied, "I did not recognise you with your clothes on."

George was another one of our oldest customers, old Dublin stock, lived right opposite Croke Park entrance, and a true gentleman. On the phone George would leave us a message, "Good morning, George here" then he would shout "Twinkle" and down went the phone. I would phone George back and tell him I booked Twinkle early on Monday for about 8am.

"Lovely," George would say, "I will have her ready over and out," and he would be gone off the phone. On one of these early mornings, I arrived at Georges and shouted "Morning," to George who waved happily and retreated indoors to get twinkle. A boyband called One

Direction was playing five nights at Croke park that week and thousands of people were walking past George's front door. George was not happy. With Twinkle in the back, I set to head back, but not before asking, "How's the concerts going George." "Ahh here," replied George. "My head is melted; they're peeing all over my garden." "Oh," I said to George, "that's not nice." "No," said George, "the sooner this one erection group bugger off the better. "Sorry George," I said with a stunned look, "One direction?" "That's them – One Erection! Not joking you Barry me garden is covered with erection fans peeing everywhere." I struggled to stop laughing but kept a straight face as I bid him farewell. See you early afternoon I cried, as I fell into the seat of the van. George waved happily. I returned to George's at one o'clock, twinkle beautiful and happy and George greeting her like she was away for a fortnight.

"Thank you, thank you," George cried and then with the payment always a fiver tip. Not content with that George gave me a bag of jellies for the trip home. "Last concert tonight George" I said, "all good after that." "Yes," said George "then I'll have to water the flowers me self." Seamus Heaney said, "you will never find the characters anywhere that you will find in Dublin." Seamus Heaney had never met George's lovely daughter Gemma, who owned Elvis. If ever a dog was well named it was Elvis. A beautiful Shih tzu with a beautiful temperament Elvis was magic. Gemma would ring or text Collette to book Elvis in.

"Tuesday Ok - Perfect" said Gemma "I'll tell him now," and Elvis was ready.

When I arrived in Coolock there was Elvis jumping up and down at the gate ready for the off, terrified in case I left without him. Settled in his cage Elvis could not wait to get to the salon. To this Elvis the

Salon was Graceland. He lapped up every moment of his grooming session. He was an absolute Joy and Collette adored him.

Back home by about 1 o'clock Elvis totally content, went to his owner to tell her all about the day he had. Gemma always rewarded us with a beautiful handmade gift of a candle or a handmade card or otherwise. In this age of cynicism and intolerance how lovely it was to find a fantastic person with a gorgeous dog. Tragically Elvis passed away recently - a shock to Gemma and a shock to us we will miss him terribly. Elvis has not gone from us He just left the building - RIP Elvis. We had another customer however who refused to leave the building and Led me a merry dance every time I went to collect her.

Elvis has just left the Building

Chapter 7
Rossie from Gormanstown

"Hi Barry - Aine here from Gormanstown."

Alarms bells rang immediately! Rossie was a beautiful Lassie Collie, an absolute joy to look at and a more even-tempered dog you could not Find. Only problem? Rossie did not like to leave home. I swear to God as soon as Aine rang to book Rossie in, he heard her. Twice I went to collect him, and he had disappeared over the fields and would not return until an hour after I left - empty handed! So when Aine rang on a Monday night I requested Aine keep him indoors so we could catch him. "No Problem Barry," says Aine, "we won't let him out in the morning!" "Great," I said to Aine, "I'll be over at 9am." "Just one thing Barry," says Aine. "Can you come in and get him because he won't even look at me for two weeks afterwards if I bring him out." "No problem Aine," I said, "I'll do that and all will be well!"

9 o'clock the next morning I arrived at the door to collect Rossie. Aine dragged me in the door and fled upstairs. I stood there bemused. "He's in the Kitchen Barry," she shouted down. "No problem," I said and into the kitchen I went. As I opened the door Rossie squeezed out the door and disappeared. "Aine, he's out of the kitchen," I shouted up the stairs. "Try the study," she replied, "He

loves it in there." To the study I went but no sign of Rossie. I left the door open and there was Rossie disappearing into the hall. "Sorry Aine," I shouted, "he's got out of the study- where to next?" With this Aine, who loved the dog and clearly did not want to get on the wrong side of him, disappeared into the bedroom. I was on my own!

I spotted an open door in the hallway and ventured in there. It was a bedroom and Rossie had sought solace under the bed. With victory in sight I dove across the bed and caught him. Rossie looked at me and laughed. Next minute a figure rose up in the bed. He looked at me, then at Rossie and fell back into the bed. I thought for a minute he was dead. It was Áine's son home for the weekend. Bemused and bewildered by the experience but thinking Business is business – I led Rossie out and headed for the front door. "Everything OK Barry?" Aine hollered down from the Bedroom. "Fine Aine," I shouted back "I've got Rossie, but I think your son might need a counsellor. "No problem Barry," Aine shouted back, "so long as Rossie is alright!"

Door opened, Rossie jumped in the cage and cage closed not a problem at all. As I went to close the door of the van I swear Rossie gave me a look as if to say, "Here, that was some craic." Yeah. If they could talk! If Rossie was reluctant to leave home, then De Nero was the exact opposite.

Chapter 8
The bigger the better

I do love large dogs - the bigger the better. German shepherds are probably my favourite breed, but Rottweilers and Labradors also feature highly, and then there's De Niro, a beautiful and statuesque Doberman who always came in for his Christmas wash and brushout – De Niro's day out. I would collect him early in the morning and he would spend the entire day with us. Never have I seen a dog enjoy a wash more than De Niro. He eyes would start to close in bliss as the sudsy water cascaded over him. He adored it. Then a long snooze under the cage dryer followed by a walk, a light lunch and then back for another forty winks before the trip home to Drogheda. De Niro was in heaven.

December 22nd came, and De Niro was booked in. I collected him as usual, and he was groomed and pampered, and we again marvelled at this beautiful animal with his super temperament. On this occasion however, we ran a bit late, so it was 6pm in the evening when I left the salon to bring De Niro home. I brought him out to set off intending to put him in the back of the Van, but De Niro spotted the open door on the passenger side of the van and hopped in. He wanted a road trip. He settled himself down on the passenger seat and waited for me to join him. "Well" I thought, "he deserves a little Christmas present," so I left him sit there and off we went. All the way to Drogheda De Niro could not take his eyes off the lit-up houses, Christmas trees and twinkling lights. He looked out at them with marvel in his eyes. Sometimes he looked at me as if to say "Thanks for this - I will never forget it."

As we approached Drogheda I spotted a Garda check point. "Crikey" I thought, "I never did my tax!" It was three weeks out of date and we had been so busy I had forgotten all about it. Not to worry I thought, most guards will give you a fool's pardon and tell you to get it sorted – basically a slap on the wrist. As we approached the guard on duty he flashed his light on the windscreen and shook his head disdainfully before coming around to me. As he took his notebook out I thought "this is not good - this young garda means business!" He tapped on the window, and I rolled it down.

"Driving licence" he barked. "Certainly" I replied, mumbling my apologies for being out of tax and explaining we had been very busy and all that. "No excuses," he barked again. "If everyone said that no tax would be paid at all." "Sorry Garda" I replied as I knew I was beginning to run out of excuses. "I could impound this van right now," he barked "and I asked you for your driving licence."

I opened the pouch under the passenger side of the van and began to rummage for my Licence. As I did this the impatient garda stuck his head in the window and shouted, "Hurry Up! I haven't got all night." As he did this De Niro - who the Garda had not spotted as he's jet black - rose up on the seat like an Egyptian God and seemed to fill the whole van. Inches from the Garda's face De Niro let out an unmerciful and very loud Woof. I had never heard De Niro bark before - not ever. I was pretty sure this was the end and began to make plans for Collette to raise the bail money. I retrieved my licence and turned around, ashen faced to address our intrepid law enforcer.

But he had obviously retreated to a safe distance. I opened the door and got out to present my licence but well, nothing. He was gone-where I have no idea.

The patrol car was gone and so was the checkpoint. Briefly I wondered if De Niro had eaten him whole, but a look in the van showed no signs of blood. I climbed back in and tentatively set off. De Niro only lived a few minutes away and he bounded out of the van and in the front door to his delighted owners. As I went to head home I turned to the owners and said, "you know folks, all the years we have been doing De Niro and I have never heard him bark once." The owner turned to me and laughed, "neither have we." Ten years and only one woof from De Niro and possibly one that saved my bacon. As I said - I just love big dogs.

De Niro, You talking to me?

Chapter 9
Charlie did not like changes

As I have already stated I love German Shepherds and Alsatians. A small dog can be a diva be it a Shitz-Zu, Bichon, or King Charles. They can wriggle and squirm and make grooming very difficult. A Yorkie will move unexpectedly at any moment, a westie can be moody, but the Shepherd and Alsatians just sit there and say, "do me." Well most of them anyway with the one exception of Charlie from Bellewstown.

Charlie did not like change at all and you had to have an empty day in the salon for Charlie. He lived in a rolling 200-acre estate and had the best of everything - food, sleeping quarters and idyllic lifestyle. He took it as an extreme inconvenience to be uprooted from all of this to be washed, groomed, de-matted and to have to spends hours away from his beloved environment. Charlie liked no-one and no other dog was tolerated. He was the Roy Keane of the dog world. No-one was allowed to be near the salon on Charlie's day out. It became known as "Charlie day." In fairness, he never snapped or growled, but you knew his message was, "Hurry up and get me home."

If Charlie was the introvert of dogs, Rebel was the exact opposite. From the moment you went to collect Rebel the experience was uplifting. He would bound out his front door and leap into the van, tail wagging and tongue sticking out. He could not wait for his wash and brush. As soon as he got to the salon it was mayhem. He was just so happy to see all the other dogs. Paws up on the table, looking at the little ones, smelling and sniffing and just cavorting madly- everything about Rebel was just pure fun.

After his wash, during which he drowned everyone in the vicinity by constantly shaking his heavy wet coat, Rebel would retire to the drying cage for a relax and a good sleep. After that he was taken to the table for a serious brushing before heading home. When he got home, he would jump out of the van, run in the front door, and drag his adoring owners out to the door to make sure they thanked me properly. They always did of course, and Rebel was always a joy to behold.

And now to Spike. If Charlie was a loner, and Rebel a socialite, then we can only describe Spike in one word - Mad! Christine, his owner was always so lovely. I would arrive at 10am and never managed to leave before 11am. "I'll put the kettle on Barry," she would shout, "just a quick Coffee maybe?" Christine's husband was not a well man. A lovely man, he was dapper and handsome, but he did not tolerate fools gladly despite always being polite. After we had our coffee Christine would say, "Alright Barry, Let's try get this lunatic in the van." Spike was a sexed-up Shepard. He was up for anything. A lovable beautiful looking Shepard and so amorous. If it moved, Spike wanted it! What I did not know however was that Spike wanted me!

On the second occasion that I collected him, Christine suggested if we brought him into the house first he might go more quietly into the van. "Right," says I, "we will give it a go." Into the house came

Spike. Christine went upstairs to check on the husband and Spike pounced - trying to disrobe me and succeeding!.

He jumped up on me and his paws were everywhere. I have to say I have experienced most things but not this. Within a minute Spike had me naked from the waist down. Dragging my tracksuit bottoms to the floor, Spike tossed them gaily above his head. I tried to grab them but Spike was having none of it. Under the table he went laughing at me. Anytime I got close he fled, happy to see me in my half naked state. Then Christine arrived back down the stairs. "God Barry! What's happened?" she cried as I stood in the middle of the kitchen trying to protect my modesty. Luckily, Spike felt sympathy for me and crawled out from under the table with half of my tracksuit bottom still intact. I climbed into them as Christine suppressed a fit of giggles. Spike happily leapt into the back of the van as we swiftly departed, ears pricked and quite happy with his last hours work. As I went to drive off out came Christine with four Louis Copeland suits over her arm. "Here Barry," she said, "I know you have a stall at Fairyhouse Market, Himself said you might get a few quid for these."

Off I went with Spike who had had his fun and listened as Collette said what a nice quiet dog he was to groom. Spike went home totally happy, looking calm, serene, and gorgeous to Christine whose eyes were still red from laughing. Before I left I said to Christine "God! Imagine if Mark had come down to find me half naked in your kitchen." Christine laughed. "Barry, he's up there having a right good laugh - I told him all about it!"

Two months later Mark passed away and Spike departed not long after. Christine went within three months, heartbroken at losing them both. Christine's Sister worked in Fairyhouse market and introduced herself to me and now I see her there every week. It feels like

Christine, Mark and Spike are with me forever, which is more than my tracksuit bottoms were that morning!

Amorous Spike

Chapter 10
They shave Jack Russell's too!

UP to fifteen years ago if you had suggested shaving Jack Russell chances are you would have been locked up. When I suggested it to people they would look at me as if I was mad and say, "But it's got no hair". They have, and plenty of it. The hair on the neck of a Jack Russell will shed everywhere, leaving a trail of hair behind them. A good shave a couple of times a year puts a stop to this and really its only in recent years that people are starting to get it.

Michelle, in Kentstown just up the road from us owns two Jack Russell's that have been coming to us for grooming for years. When they arrived at first, they would look at you bewildered as to what the hell you were doing to them and once groomed, would bark incessantly to get out of the madhouse. Over the years they seem to have learned to accept their fate and now actually enjoy their day out, to the extent that when Michelle went on holidays they stayed with us for the week and not a bother did they give all week. Jackers are a very adaptable dog and when you get to know them, they are a very loyal and affectionate animal.

Sandy is another one who comes to us every year and stays for a month. A tiny Jack Russell is Sandy but with a mighty presence. Sandy knows that come July he must leave his home in Bettystown and come to reside at his holiday residence. He does not bat an eyelid at the move but struts in, inspects his quarters and then after a brief snack, bullets outside to let our own dogs know that Sandys back in town. Just a marvellous character is Sandy.

Around the corner is Poppy, a lovely even tempered Jacker, whose eyes start to close in bliss once in the bath. She loves the hot water and adores the cage dryer afterwards. She leaves you in no doubt that this is Poppy time.

People think that Jack Russell's don't need grooming, but they are entitled to a pamper too and it's amazing what a good wash and brush out can do for a seemingly hairless dog. One such dog was the beautiful Daisy who came to us for years. Twice a year her owner Muriel would have Daisy in for a day out. I would collect her and just sit her on the front seat with me - there was no "back of the van" for this lady. Once in the salon, a long wash which Daisy loved would be followed by a brush out and along luxurious nap – Daisy was in pure heaven.

One morning I collected Daisy for her day out I sat her in the front as usual but there was something different about her that I could not put my finger on. Once back at the salon, she did not seem to enjoy the wash as much as usual and while drying, where Daisy would usually lap it up she remained standing on all fours as though she was trying to tell us something.

Not happy, Collette gathered her up and we made for the vets, which was only minutes away. I rang Muriel to tell her what was happening and once at the Vets Daisy was put on a drip. It transpired that Daisy had only been to the vets a few days beforehand and it appeared that whatever medication she had been given had triggered a reaction, but we will never know for sure as shortly after Muriel arrived, Daisy unfortunately died. Collette and I were heartbroken, so the lord alone knows how Muriel felt knowing her faithful companion of years was gone. Most of our days are filled with smiling dogs and wagging tails and Happy Endings - this was not. It was one of the saddest days we ever had since opening. Thankfully, it was a rare one and we would recover.

And after a while so did Muriel. She is now the proud owner of Scruffy, a lovable terrier whom we also have the pleasure of grooming regularly and who is Muriel's constant companion. After Daisy passed, Muriel made a beautiful gesture, leaving a bouquet of flowers at our door, thanking us for all we had done for Daisy. No drama no fuss just pure Muriel. Form as they say, is temporary, but Class is permanent.

Chapter 11
Even groomers need Holidays

"We are off to Egypt," I announced to a startled Collette. "Where?" she queried, a shocked look spreading across her face. "Yep" I informed her. "Egypt - well Luxor to be precise." Why? Because after three years of hard work building up a business we deserved a holiday. I had spotted a great deal in Drogheda Travel agents window, very cheap because it was St. Patricks weekend, and I took it upon myself to book it. "But why not Spain, or Portugal? Why Egypt?" Collette asked. "Ah No!" I replied, "too boring for us. Tutankhamun, The Sphinx, Cleopatra, the land of the Pharaohs." I was beginning to bluster, and I could see I was not convincing her. Still a week later we were off on our way for a week of relaxation in the hot Egyptian sun.

After a long flight and a bus trip we arrived in Luxor. We booked into our hotel, had a beautiful room, and were served a fine dinner and any doubts of my choice started to fade. Next morning being an early riser I went on an exploration mission in Luxor. I was shocked. Poverty was evident everywhere as were multiple beggars - this was not something I was prepared for. The opulence of the Hotel we were staying in and the marvellous food we were experiencing not to mention the rooftop pool and plush sunbathing area surrounding it were in stark contrast to the squalor that existed outside the hotel.

As I returned to the hotel a young man asked if we were interested in a tour to the Valley of the Kings. "You will see the real Egypt," he promised, "not the overpriced excursion that the Hotel does, but real people in their villages, through the desert and to my family home for dinner." I jumped on this amazing offer and raced upstairs to impart this wonderful news to a half-awake Collette. The next morning at 7am we went downstairs to meet our guide outside the hotel as arranged. Well enthused I let him know we were ready as I looked around for our transport. "This way," he said, leading us around the corner and there was our luxury vehicle – a horse and cart. He cheerfully hopped into the driver's seat ushering us into the passenger seats directly behind him. I think both of us were in a trance as we climbed aboard the carts rickety frame. All aboard, a flick of the whip and we were off.

In fairness our guide Samir had promised us we would experience the real Egypt and we saw that all right. Once out of Luxor and into the desert, we travelled through several small communities. Most had self-made straw huts for homes with mud holding them together and open fires burning outside them. Children ran alongside our cart cheering and waving to us with gusto, some even trying to board the cart but received a crack of the whip from Samir as a deterrent. I think he reckoned that the extra load might just pull the cart apart!

The last village we passed through was set on a tributary of the river Nile, with a larger group of people bathing it in. Samir stopped and pointed them out to us. He pulled up close to them. It was the first village we were not cheered or waved at in so they must have had something more interesting afoot I thought. And they had. They were pulling a baby Crocodile looped in ropes out of the river, men, women and children pulling it to the riverbank before displaying their big game trophy to us amid loud cheers. Suitably impressed, we drove on.

At one point we had to cross a border check point close to our destination. As we approached it I did wonder how Samir would negotiate it. Stern looking Israeli Soldiers fully armed and unsmiling spoke with him, then looked to us as we smiled nervously back. One by one they saw the funny side of something and broke into smiles before waving us through. I think they came to the conclusion that we were mad! An hour later we arrived at our destination.

We went to enter the Valley of the Kings, anticipation high and eyes full of wonder, like school children on a school trip. We turned back to look for Samir who we thought was following behind us, only to realise he had vanished. I went back to the entrance to find him. He was sitting under a tree, Mr Ed the donkey lying in the shade beside him. He was not allowed in. No our guide was not welcome we were told by officials, and I quizzed them as to why he could not enter having brought us all this way. Only tourists could enter they said, and as I protested Samir just smiled and waved us in. "Enjoy," he called, "I will be here when you come back."

"But what if he isn't?" I said to Collette, "how will we get back? There are no taxis in the desert."

"We are here," she said "so let's just see it, and by the way we haven't given him any money yet, so I don't think he will go home empty handed." Common sense prevailed and we went in.

It was an amazing experience. Human forms preserved over thousands of years, including a small baby wrapped in swaddling cloth. This was not for generally for public viewing we were told by the official unless we wanted to contribute a few Euros to the upkeep of the tomb. I gave him a few coins which I naturally was not familiar with, and he quickly pocketed them, then opened the case to unveil a perfectly formed baby which he told us was to have been a future King but died in infancy. We spent over three hours in the valley of the Kings, and it remains to this day one of the most interesting experiences of our lives. It gave us the impetus to visit many other countries of historical interest in the following years.

As we left the valley we both felt that this was something special, as if we had seen something that really mattered and that would stay with us forever. Samir and Mr. Ed were totally refreshed on our return, and he quickly hitched up the cart and we were on our way back. The guards at the checkpoint once again shook their heads incredulously as we passed and waved us through with a few smiles. Samir told us we would be back within two hours, and he lit up a cigarette, probably to celebrate our safe return. Collette and I both liked the odd cigarette so when he offered us one of these magic cigarettes as he called them we both took the attitude, "when in Rome" and took the proffered cigarettes. An hour later Samir burst into song which echoed all over the desert and twenty minutes later he was still going. Collette, who is face at this stage resembled Marianne Faithful during her Rolling Stone era joined in and their voices rang out loud and clear in the emptiness of the Sahara. Our guide was stoned and so was my wife! I think even Mr Ed was a little ropey!

Twenty minutes later Collette demanded we stop for food. Hells bells I thought she's got the munchies. Samir pulled up outside a swanky looking outpost and we disembarked. As we entered a strict looking manager approached and welcomed us warmly but told Samir he could not enter. "No problem," Samir shouted, "I'll wait for you out here."

We had spent the whole day in the charming boy's company and no way were we entertaining that. "What's up," I said, "he's with us and he's hungry too." "No, no, no." replied the manger "He cannot come in." "Then we won't either," I snarled at the manger. "Goodbye." Samir was surprised to see us so quickly. We told him we had started the journey together and would finish it together. I looked at his face and I think he was really moved by this. He really did not expect anyone to stand up to the bullying the way we had – he just accepted it. The manager came over to us again and offered his most sincere apologies. "Big mistake, so sorry so sorry" he bawled. And back in we went - together.

Collette and I ordered salads with cold meats while Samir had two hamburgers and chips and ate them rapidly, looking like a child in Butlins. He drank his coke in a minute followed by three more in another few minutes before we left. Collette had only eaten half her salad and Samir demolished the rest followed by a chocolate pudding desert to finish off, before resuming his position in the driver's seat of the cart. We pulled up outside the hotel twenty minutes later and Samir suggested we visit his family for dinner the next night instead of tonight as promised – he was just stuffed! We left him with a sizable tip for which he lovingly kissed Collette in appreciation, but he never kissed me. We left him fed, rich and happy and promised to see him over the coming days but we never did. Seven days in Luxor is a short time and with a lot to see, not to mention a day to recover from the best road trip of my life. When we got home we said we would go back again, and we did several times. Not back to Luxor but to Sharm El Sheik and we had many great holidays in that fabulous country. Over the years we explored Tunisia, Morocco, Turkey, and Hungary. We have visited the Grand Canyon in Nevada, Hollywood in L.A., the Empire State Building in New York, and Table Mountain in South Africa. Even China's Beijing has not eluded us. But it all started in Luxor - that's where our eyes were opened and where our taste for travel began. With a guy called Samir and a Horse called Ed!

Chapter 12
Jingle Bells Doggy style

From December 12th until Christmas eve, the phone would never stop ringing. All our regulars' dogs had to have their Christmas spruce up in preparation for Santa. From December 17th we worked well into the night to make sure all our little charges were sorted. I was on the road from six in the morning until sometimes ten o clock at night. People took full advantage to do their Christmas shopping while the pooch was getting his or her special makeover. "I'll be back about three," I would say only to be asked, "Could you make it a bit later - I have a bit of shopping to do." A lot of our regulars would pay me as I collected their fur babies and some we would give me a key or leave it under the mat saying, "Just throw him in the door Barry." Their trust never ceased to amaze me as did their generosity on my return, even if not there. A bottle of fine wine, a box of Dairy Milk or Roses and a card with, "thank for Everything over the year" always gave me such a feel-good vibe. Even the dogs seemed to know it was Christmas.

If not, they certainly sensed that something was different. With tails wagging furiously and big happy grins on their furry faces I would swear they knew that Santa Dog was coming too. To this day I can remember their faces in the Christmas cookie perfumed salon the way Charles Donut remembers his boys in the film "Goodbye Mr.

Chips." There was Eileen's dog Harry whom we groomed for years-a truculent Westie who fought Collette for years before giving in to his fate but over time he became a lamb. Harry always arrived after a digging experience in his back garden. He would always be black with dirt, so we christened him Dirty Harry after the Clint Eastwood film. Max, a handsome King Charles spaniel was another regular who came from Ratoath and was always very horny. He loved the ladies, and the ladies loved him. To Max the grooming was just an extra - the chance of a pull was the main event. A wonderful temperament and a smashing character all the ladies loved him, and we did too.

On a Sunday morning in Fairyhouse Max's owner Sharon would bring him over for a walk and usually stopped by the stall for a chat. Max nearly broke the leash trying to get to me. "Ah would you look at that," gushed Sharon as she looked on amazed. "He just loves Barry," she would inform other customers as Max strained to get closer to me. Max did love me, but I think he more loved the fact that every two months I would arrive at his home and bring him to what he was sure was the best little brothel in Meath.

There was Paddington, a lovely Shih tzu, who sauntered into the salon, got groomed and sauntered home again. Every day was a ground hog day to Padders - no matter where he was his motto was relax and he sure as hell did.

Agatha and Captain - talk about Chalk and cheese - this was a classic case. Agatha a pompous beautiful Pomeranian and Captain an ebullient gorgeous Greyhound who would literally lick you to death. They were totally different but devoted to each other.

Rusty and Spike from Drogheda were among our first customers and two of Collette's favourite ever adorable Yorkies, who would cry if they could not see each other. Collette would sometimes groom them at the same time and there is no more adorable sight than two tea-cup Yorkies sitting quietly on the grooming table awaiting their makeover.

Then we had Willow a beautiful Spaniel who had to be carried to the van kicking and screaming by her owner and once there all he would do was sleep. Not one for socialising was Willow. The last time I brought him home I had another Spaniel in the back. "Ah," said Sinead, "Gorgeous as usual and look he's got a little friend." I looked at Sinead and said, "Willow does not do friends." "No," says Sinead, "I'm afraid not." "The Bob Dylan of dogs is our Willow," I said. Sinead laughed heartily and said, "not to worry he still looks gorgeous and I love him." "As do we all," I said and so we do.

Then there was Gizmo who only lived around the corner, Another stunning Pom who loved being groomed but hated leaving his home. As soon as I arrived to collect Gizmo, he looked out the window, saw the van and fled. "Barry," says the exhausted owner, "I can't get him – will you try?"

And in I went, under beds, behind the couch, all round the Kitchen - Gizmo hid everywhere. As soon as I got close to him he was gone again, barking loudly, and giving an impish grin at my flailing efforts to catch him. Eventually Gizmo got tired, and I managed to corral him. And when I did he just looked at me sheepishly and gave me the Gizmo grin. It wasn't that Gizmo disliked me, he just wanted to have a bit of fun. In the saloon he retreated for a long snooze after his run-around and sometimes I wished I could join him. We called this the Gizmo workout! A marvellous character who would go home beautiful, happy, and content. Before bounding into his home Gizmo would look at me knowingly and I swear he was saying, "Till next time Bud." If only they could talk!

Casanova Max

Chapter 13
So what am I really?

I have been involved with dogs all my life from my farming days, over thirty years ago to today where my job title or status is what? I'm not a dog groomer as I don't have the qualifications, so I guess I'm just the one who collects and brings them home. So what am I really? I asked Collette one day and she just laughed and shrugged it off. "Does it really matter?" she said. "Not really I suppose," I answered but I still wondered. And then one day I found out exactly what I was.

On an early morning call for Pluto in Stamullen I was there at 7am and not unusually the household was asleep. I knocked and rang with no reply, so I tried again. A young girl of not more than 7 or 8 opened the door, obviously up early. "Hi" I said, "I'm here to collect Pluto." "yeah Barry," she said, "hold on and I'll get him." A shout from mammy upstairs inquires who it is. "It's alright Mammy" was the reply "It's only the doggy man!" Well that cheered me up no end – at least I know what I am. I relayed the story to my old friend Leo in the Stags over a pint that evening. "Imagine that," I said, "some people refer to me as the bloody doggy man." Leo looked at me and smiled. "Don't know what you are getting excited about," he said, "sure people have been calling you that for years." "Well thanks for telling me Leo," says I. "Look on the bright side," said Leo. "What bright side?" I asked. "Well," he exclaimed, "Imagine what they would be calling you if you were collecting Cats!" I quite happily settled for my title then.

We are entering our 16th year in business and so thankful to be still in business. Many thanks are due to our marvellous owners who trust us with their beautiful dogs - their babies. It never fails to amaze me the kindness and gratitude these people show us. No matter where I go, all I ever feel is happiness when I bring their pooch home. There are exceptions of course but very few. We are not perfect – no one is – and sometimes people are not happy with the results of what we might have had to do. But to us the dog comes first and the only guarantee we can give is that the dogs will get the care and attention they need as a priority. Sometimes at Fairyhouse people shout at me "howdy Barry" and I look at them stupidly, knowing the face but not remembering the name. Then they shout out Buster, Bella, Tyson, or other dogs name and as soon as they do I twig who they are straight away. Without these people our Business does not exist and without these people and their beautiful pooches our everyday joy in grooming dogs would not be possible. And without these people this book would never have been written.

Chapter 14
If only they could Bite

"Fran Toner here Barry," roared Fran. "Howya," I replied to one of the most decent people I've ever met. A complete gentleman and a character to boot, Fran didn't suffer fools gladly - A spade was a spade - and one always knew where one stood with Fran. He had a fearsome reputation for being hard, granite like and unbending. I always found Fran likeable, friendly, and loyal - a true friend. "Dog here needs to be groomed," Barry Fran bellowed. "Right" says I "What have you got?" "A Springer Spaniel," Fran growled. "Lovely" I said, "always such a nice friendly dog." "Not this one," said Fran. "It would ambush you given a half a chance!" I laughed it off - "they all say that Fran. I'm sure he can't be that bad." He WAS!

From the moment Fran's dog squirmed into the van until he got home was hell. Fran had warned us and by God he was right. We got him washed all right but from the moment he got on the grooming table all the wanted was blood - anyone's blood! For three hours we ducked, dodged and weaved around him before finally getting him groomed much to his disgust. Into the van immediately and home with him I went. I arrived at Fran and he was delighted with the results. "He is a handful," I said to Fran. "Oh God yeah," Fran agreed. "I tried clipping him once myself, but he wasn't having it. No way. He bit me twice and then ate the clippers." "Great thanks," I said, "so you sent him up to me!" "Ah" said Fran, "sure isn't that what you are paid for!

Toffee was a smashing looking little cross who hated men. From house to cage and from cage to saloon it was women only. Collette had to retrieve Toffee from the van, and once groomed and dried had to return him to the van. Once home again Toffee demanded female handling only. Toffee was a complete feminist. In his later years Toffee relented a little and now I have gained a little trust with him. He will let me bring him out to the saloon and back to the van to bring home. But would I trust him? Not an inch!

Spider dog Jesse was another legend in the saloon. Collette could shave her no bother although for the face she squirmed a bit, but we managed. However washing - no way Jesse hated water. At one stage we washed Jesse as she hung by her nails from the ceiling in her efforts to avoid the hose. She would not tolerate water. It was like fighting an octopus, she fought you all the way. She just hated it! Once washed Jesse would calm down and once in the drier went to sleep before home. Sometimes difficult was Jesse, but another character gone and sorely missed.

And then there was Rosie and what a handful she was. We assumed Rosie was banned from every groomer within a 30-mile radius. Some dogs have a quirk about something, their face, some their feet and others their tails. Rosie hated everything. Sometimes I had to collect her myself from the backyard and she even hated that. Darting around her domain, ducking, and diving behind anything that resembled cover Rosie led me one hell of a dance. Sometimes I would have to resort to a lasso technique, stalking Rosie with the lead twirling in my hand looking like an extra in a John Wayne film, as Rosie went from behind the bins to the back of her kennel.

Eventually and luckily I would get her into the back of the van, kicking and screaming and then back to the salon.

Having not wanted to get into the van now Rosie did not want to get out. She knew where she was going all right. After a lot of coaxing and cajoling and a fierce resistance, Rosie was in the salon. Now the fun began. Squirming and twisting like a jellied eel, Rosie would allow a certain amount of grooming before turning with a snap or a snarl to let Collette know she was not a happy dog. After what seemed an age Rosie was done a fine testament to Collette's grooming skills and extreme patience. Next up was the wash with no let up from Rosie. She hated it. Water was not her friend and we had washed St Bernard dogs in the half the time it took to wash her. Into the drier and at last something Rosie liked. She would lie like a lamb, snoozing but with one eye open, in case we were about to inflict any more torture on her. Drying complete Rosie would go the van without any resistance- she knew she was going home. Once Rosie was back on her stomping ground she pranced around looking a million dollars, and as I left she would look at me with an evil smile as if to say, "next time I'll make it even harder for you! There was a feeling of Triumph when I left Rosie's that almost match the feeling of despair when I went to collect her. Belligerent, cantankerous and sometimes downright bold, Rosie was pure bad ass. Famous statement from film star James Mason "All the ladies love a bad guy, and all the guys love a bad girl"- I guess that's why we loved Rosie.

Rosie the Salon Demon

Chapter 15
Pampered pooches and other furry boarders

"I need someone to mind my Pepe," said Mrs O'Leary to me at the market on a sunny Sunday morning. "It will be only 5 days, but I can't put him in the kennels." I could understand that. Pepe was a 7-year-old poodle, blind as a bat and needy as hell. "I can't trust him with anyone except you Barry," she said. "Sorry Mrs O," I replied. "we don't actually mind dogs." Totally dismayed she began to walk away. "You would not find me ungenerous," she said, "whatever it takes." "No" I said "it's nothing to do with money. We are just not set up for it." "But you have poodles yourself," she answered. "Yes," says I, "five of them." "Then one more would not be that big an inconvenience. He is so good and once he has his Rich Tea biscuits, he will be good as gold"

Once again I declined saying he was a big responsibility. "Mum needs a holiday, and this is the only chance I have to bring her away," she cried, "What will I do." My arm was being twisted. "But listen," I said, "We would never forgive ourselves if anything happened to him." "But it won't," she cried. "He loves you and Collette." "I can't do it," I said. "We love Pepe but it's just too big a responsibility." She shuffled off despondently.

I felt bad because Pepe really was a darling to us. I must have looked downcast because Collette asked me what was wrong. I told her about the conversation, and she said "But why? Pepe would be no problem. We will mind her." "What?" I replied, "the responsibility and all that." "Where is she?" she asked and I pointed stupidly to where I reckoned Mrs O'Leary might be, but she was gone.

Collette shook her head disdainfully and went off for her morning tea and doughnuts, firing a glance of disgust in my direction. Mrs O'Leary arrived back just after she left so I called her and informed her of the joint decision Collette had made. Joy was not the word to describe her face. You would have thought she had won the lotto.

Pepe was coming to stay and any fears of a fragile "handle with care" dog soon disappeared. When not cavorting with our own poodles, he would stride majestically around her new surroundings, sniffing out the best spots for an hour or twos kip. Although totally blind, Pepe would sit on the couch for hours staring out the window. If anyone passed the window be it postman, binman or a stray cat, Pepe would kick off barking furiously to let us know of a possible intruder. At bedtime Pepe had to have rich tea biscuits which Collette had to soak in tea first. Sometimes we would try him on unsoaked biscuits but he wasn't having that. Tea-soaked biscuits or none at all, and one was never enough - it had to be half a dozen or so. Pepe adored his rich tea biscuits.

When he went home to his owner the house seemed very quiet. For a 17-year-old inactive disabled and fragile dog he sure left his mark on us. And several packets of Rich Tea biscuits!

We had just inherited Impala, a beautiful mischievous young Shih tzu who loved fun and devilment. We rescued him before he was moved to kennels and he joined our own troop, settling in immediately. Impala had boundless energy and at times you would look at our own aging crew lying outstretched in the sun while Impala tried to rouse them. Impala always greeted the dogs who would come for grooming with a raucous yelp and would leap around madly hoping they had come to play. Around this time the owners of Cassie, a smashing looking cross breed asked if we would mind her for a week while they went on holidays.

Cassie arrived and came in like a wrecking ball, full of vitality, cavorting madly around our outdoor area. Impala fell in love immediately, almost breaking the gate to join her, so we let him in. Impala was doctored so that wasn't a problem.

The joy of looking at two young dogs playing together was pure pleasure. They absolutely adored each other. Wrestling like lunatics seemed to be their greatest fun as they yelped in delight while rolling around madly. Pure pleasure.

On one occasion, while grooming on a summer afternoon with the window of the salon wide open onto our outdoor area we heard an unmerciful growling and grunting so we quickly rushed out to see what was going on. We had a kennel in that area and Impala had decided it would be a good idea to leap from the top of it. He had climbed up and jumped, landing on Cassie's back. Cassie thought this was a super idea and was doing likewise. We watched in amazement as the two dogs bounced happily off each other before retiring for an hour's kip in the afternoon sun, after which they resorted to a spot of doggie wrestling - two dogs in heaven.

Cassie returned home after her week and in the mornings Impala would bound out only to discover Cassie gone. He would stare forlornly into the empty outdoor area before skulking away and lying down with his head on his paws. Impala was depressed because his love had left him. After a few days he would start to rouse the poodles again and sometimes they would engage but they could never make up for Cassie. Luckily, Cassie spends a lot of time with us and when she comes to stay the pure joy on Impala's face is unreal. I would swear that Cassie feels the same way. Cassie's owners always say to her, "you are going to Barry's" and she starts wagging her tail and dancing in circles. "Oh, she loves Barry," they tell everyone, but I think it's because she is going to see Impala, her soulmate. Over the years Impala has become the perfect host dog and loves to see other dogs arriving to stay. He will play with them for hours on end and they seem to love him as well. Some dogs don't and just want their own company but most of them fall for Impalas charm. Its Cassie he loves the most though, his first and maybe only love and the only one he gets sad about when she leaves. It's all about Cassie, the rest are only conversation.

"Barry" said Sue "mum won't go on holidays unless you mind Charlie. How are you fixed?"

The dates were good so mum could go and Charlie was coming to stay. A big proud good-humoured Boxer, who was up for a regular wash all year round, we knew Charlie well. Sue who was Paddington's owner, told me her mum came across Charlie one day as he was about to be killed. The local Travellers had owned Charlie and because of his let's say ordinary foolish and ungrateful ways were getting rid of him. Sue's mum had happened across him and told the Travellers she would take him. They wanted cash for his life, which she duly paid.

Charlies was saved and went home to live with this diamond of a lady. The day before she went away I was collecting Charlie, who sensed he was going somewhere. As I packed his food, bed and toys and brought him home he looked at me knowing this was different than the usual grooming. An hour out the back with Impala and Charlie was happy. They tired each other out and it was late evening when Impala fell into bed in his usual spot. Charlie conked out on the salon floor and never moved until 6 o'clock the next morning. As I went in he got up stretched and with Impala jumping at the window, pawed at the door to be let outside to join him. A lovable nut he jumped up on me and cried outside freedom. As he did this he crouched for a moment, straddled and with the legs spread wide apart unleashed an unmerciful fart. I laughed but not for long - the smell was potent. The remains of it were still there when Collette came in. "Oh my god," she said "what in the name of god is that?" she said covering her face. Charlie leapt up at the salon window grinning his joker faced smile as if to say, "Ha-ha." Outside all day with Impala, Charlies farting never really impacted on us and didn't seem to bother Impala either. But after his feed every evening and a good night's sleep, first thing in the morning Charlie would let loose, then smile at you, as happy as if he were performing at Crufts.

The night before he went home I was outside fixing a paving slab in the outdoor area. Charlie had decided to have a late night and was outside with me scrutinising my efforts. Head beside me, he would look quizzically at me almost asking what I was doing. As I finished off, I rose form my crouch and said loudly to Charlie who was standing behind me, "thank God that's done." "Took you long enough" said Charlie.

Stunned, I looked around as he stood there grinning at me. I was frozen like a statue as I stood there looking at him. "What did you say?" I mumbled stupidly looking at Charlie. "I said about time too," said Collette who was looking out the Salon window and had been observing me for ten minutes. "Let's get Dinner." A few weeks later I saw Sue who told me her mother had a great time in France and never worried once about Charlie. "Delighted," I said. "Yeah," said Sue, "she has to go into hospital next week. Nothing serious, just a bit of a nose problem. Her sense of smell has gone." That answered everything for me. A fine gorgeous farting boxer belonging to a lady who can't smell much, a match made in heaven. And by the way I am still recovering from the shock of thinking it was Charlie answering me that night. I would not have been least bit surprised if it had been.

Chapter 16
Who's dog is it anyway?

We all make mistakes and mine was a real beauty. Let me explain. I had a Friday morning 9-o-clock pick up in Drogheda. A lovely Shih tzu called Chaz, followed by a 10.30 in Ashbourne - another Shih tzu called Billy, both black and white and both super friendly. After grooming both were snoring happily in their cages as the drier did its work. Two hours later it was time to go home so into the van and off we set. I remarked to Collette that they might as well be brothers as they looked so alike. "Yes," she said, "but you can always tell who is who." I couldn't!

I went to Ashbourne first, opened the van and said "home Billy," as he leapt into my arms. I carried him to the front door and his owner Maria made a great fuss of him as he bounded in the door. And so off to Drogheda with Shaz, whose owner Karin was in the garden as she often was and retrieved Shaz form the van herself. "Ah he looks gorgeous," she said as he toddled inside. "Great Karin," I said, "see you in a few months." I drove off happily. Later that evening Maria rang to ask if we had fed Billy at the Salon as he had not touched his food which was very unlike him. "Not sick is he?" I asked but she replied, "Oh No, he's happy as Larry, looks gorgeous and is gone for a snooze right now." "Right" says I "if I think of anything I will give you a ring back." An hour later Shaz' owner Karin rang to thank

Collette for the wonderful job done on her dog. "He is lying by the fire snoring his head off she said. It's very unusual for him as normally he would not be one for the heat." "Evenings are still cold," I said to Karin. "Maybe losing his coat made him feel a bit nippy." "Ah," said Karin, "that is probably it. Thank Collette again. Tell her he's like a different dog."

Phone off I turned to Collette to tell her Karin had rung and was delighted with Shaz, "Like a different dog she said." Like a different dog. No wonder. He was a different dog. "She's got Billy" I cried, and Maria has Shaz" as Collette looked at me in horror. "I better ring," I said to Collette. "And what?" said Collette, "have them worry all night? No. Both dogs are safe and comfortable. We will sort it out in the morning. There is no damage done. Really." I guess she was right, the dogs were not in danger so in the morning I would explain everything and look like a complete idiot. I would be the laughingstock of the canine world. I never slept a wink that night. Collette slept like an angel.

Next morning, I was on the road to Drogheda and pulled up at Karins at 7.30am. She looked surprised to see me. "Barry, did you leave something behind you?" she asked. Billy ran out and jumped into the back of the van. "Ah look" said Karin "he wants to go with you again." No, I thought to myself, Billy wants to go home. "Collette sent me down. Said she forgot to do his nails." "Really" exclaimed Karin. "There was no need for you to come down. Sure he could get them clipped next time."

All part of the service Karin. I am afraid Collette is a perfectionist and would not be happy knowing the job was not finished." "Ah Barry" she said, "that's why we always use Le Paws, professional to the last." If only she knew!. Up to Ashbourne and knocked at Marias door, who also looked a little surprised. "Just checking on Billy," I said. "Not a bother on him Barry look." And sure enough there was Shaz, tucking into his breakfast. "Nails," I replied, "Collette forgot to do his nails." "Oh Right but no need. His nails never give him any trouble. He'll be fine". "No, no" I retorted "Nails are very important. Need to have them checked." "Well if you are sure?" said Maria "I really don't want to put you to any trouble." "No trouble at all," I replied. "All part of the service." She gathered Shaz in her arms and as I put him in the van I put a spare collar around his neck. Shaz looked at me in amusement before settling down for what he thought was going to be a long snooze.

Minutes later I was back in the salon, both dogs back where they had started 24 hours earlier. Relief flowed through me like a death row prisoner who had just got a stay of execution. An hour later, both dogs washed again and lying comfortably in their cages, Shaz with a pink collar it was time for home again. Collette had put two doggie bows around their necks. No mistakes this time she said. I was taking no chances. I put Shaz in the van on his own and hightailed it for Drogheda. Returned to the haven of his own home, his delighted owner admired his bow and the freshly clipped nails, telling me what a wonderful service we provided. Back to collect Billy and off to Ashbourne with Billy in the cage. I knocked on Maria door and she was delighted to take him back so quickly. In went Billy and ran to his empty bowl, Shaz having devoured it earlier. "Look at him," said Maria, "back to his old self, hungry as usual. I must admit Barry I was a little worried last night when he did not eat." "Really," I stuttered "He seems alright now." "Ah yes," she said, "you would swear he was a different dog." I fled!

Chapter 17
Beautiful Ali the retriever

A regular visitor Ali brought us all so much joy throughout the years. Hated being washed but loved to be brushed and when finished would lazily sleep until it was time to go home. Just an all-round gorgeous dog was Ali. After years of grooming Ali's owners told us they were having to let he go as her hair was causing havoc with their sons' asthma. They asked if we knew anyone who would take her. Ali was 10 years old, and this was going to be very difficult, almost impossible. And that's exactly how it turned out to be. It began to look as if Ali was heading to the kennels. Collette was looking at me and I knew that look. "We can't let her go to the kennels," and the two boys chimed in behind her. Both loved Ali as much as we did. "No," I said firmly. "This is not our problem. We already have 6 dogs; we cannot give her what she needs." "We can," they protested. "Ali is different." I stood my ground, as they looked at me as if I had abandoned her myself.

But I was emphatic. No it was not practical. That was until 6-o-clock that evening when I was on my way to Bettystown to collect Ali. She looked a bit bemused as I arrived, her look saying, "a bit late in the day for this isn't it?" But she jumped into the back of the van smiling as usual as we set off.

As I arrived back all three of the rescuers were standing at the front of the Salon and cheered as Ali sauntered into the house. It was like a scene from the Waltons. Next morning Ali got up, stretched, and followed me into the salon. She looked at the bath and then looked at me with horror in her eyes. They had given me a large blanket that Ali had used previously, and I put it in the corner of the salon. Ali sniffed it and then lay on it looking at me as if to say "Breakfast?" I duly obliged and she ate heartily before closing her eyes for a snooze. Ali was home. The joy Ali brought us was all was beautiful Never was there a dog who could radiate affection like Ali. She oozed it. As soon as dinner started cooking Ali smelled it, leaving her comfort zone to wander in the back door to see if there were any rich pickings for her. Never disappointed. Over the years any dog arriving for grooming was sniffed and nosed at, to make sure they made the requirements and then back to her blanket she went. Ali was the perfect salon dog.

Now Charlie the boxer could fart, but he was not in Ali's league. Ali did not just fart, she used her big tail to waft it around everywhere. And it sure as hell was pungent. Then she would look at us as if to say it wasn't her. Some evenings in winter Ali would wander in after grooming finished for the day and lie in front of the fire. The grandkids would set their toys on top of her and look on amazed as she never even moved. As I said Ali was a beautiful creature, a one-off dog I don't believe I will ever see the like of again. She took bad and we brought her to the vet. Ali was riddled with cancer they had to put her to sleep. I stood beside her as they did, and Ali looked at me and smiled, "you saved me once but you can't do anything this time," and she quietly went to sleep. Thank god Collette and the boys bullied me that day as eight years of loveliness came from that dog.

None of us will ever forget that always smiling, always happy, always loving and always dog. Ali RIP

Ali Come Home

Chapter 18
You're sniffed!

A beautiful Springer Spaniel Chip arrived up to us sixteen years after we began grooming. Chip was a sniffer dog at Dublin airport, whose handler Linda also had Jessie a gorgeous retriever who was with us for years. Jessie got washed, trimmed, and dried and then slept until it was time for home, a typical retriever. Chip on the other hand was alert, hyper and inquisitive and sniffed and nosed everything until he went home. Collette once said if ever a dog was born for grooming it was Chip. Whatever she asked of him he did. "Down Chip," "Up Chip," Leg Up Chip," – whatever the command he did it immediately. "A groomers Joy," declared Collette. Once finished Chip would give her a big sloppy kiss as if to say thank you. Just the one mind. Chip was too controlled to give anything more. On the return home Jessie would saunter into the house without any fuss. Chip would leap out of the van, a quick tail wag, a quiet smile as if to say, "well done. Excellent job, Bye," before heading into his beloved owner. Chip was not one for expressing his feelings. Except once.

We returned late one night to Dublin airport from Tunisia on a full flight and with plenty of passengers carrying a few packets of cigarettes more than the allowed quota. After collecting our bags, we headed for the customs hall, when all of a sudden a few cries went up from the passengers in front of us. A truculent Springer Spaniel was bolting towards us. He stopped at Collette, wagged his tail, gave us his big Chipper smile, and leapt up on Collette. He planted his customary big Licky kiss on her. Just the one mind. Chip was still in control. Linda came after him. "So sorry guys," Linda said "He saw you Collette and slipped off his lead. So unlike him." The other passengers looked on thinking this was either a serious bust or a romantic love story.

As we went through passport control Chip was standing to attention by Linda, nose twitching, ever alert and back in the zone. A month later Jessie and Chip were up for grooming. Jessie as usual sleepily putting up with her overexertion's, Chip obedient as always. As Collette finished off Chip with her customary, "now Chippie you are ready for home," Chip gave her his customary big kiss, except this time he gave two, as if to say, "Sorry for the carry-on last month." And then off the table he leapt and adopted his usual soldier's stance. Chip was back in control.

Chapter 19
Covid comes to town

Ten years of long days and nights stopped in March 2020. The country closed down. Covid was here. I have lived through quite a lot in my life but never a pandemic. For three weeks it was case of who would kill who first in the house. In an environment of constant activity suddenly we had nothing to do and we could feel it. Temperamental cases (one was me) and one who could ration things out, this was a case of who flipped first. Knife edge stuff.

Sunday morning, I got into the van to go to the shop, just to know what it felt like to be collecting again. Returning home, a blue light behind me pulled me in. A garda walked up and from a safe distance bellowed at me. "Barry are you collecting Dogs?" "Of course not," I replied, "sure we are not allowed to." "Bollocks," he replied, "essential services. Get your arse down to my mother's tomorrow and collect Milo. He is as hairy as shite and she is cracking up." "Restrictions," I replied stupidly. "Essential services," he cried again. "What time will I tell her?" "7:30am" I said. "I'll ring her now," he replied. "What if I'm stopped?" I said. "You won't be," he answered. "Any problems refer them to me."

Next morning I felt like a bird released. I was at Milo's at 7am. His owner was up and ready and never have I seen such a delighted owner. As for Milo, a troublesome Westie cross, I never loved seeing a dog as much. "Hours later and Milo was heading home. I hit a checkpoint where the garda took a quick look at the sign on the van, gave me a big smile and waved us through. So delighted was the owner to have her baby done, I was sent home with the fees and a huge brambly apple tart. Back through the checkpoint receiving good natured waves and nods of well done and I returned home. We had lift off. From the phone calls we had to request grooming the next day I was in three counties and 12 towns. This was fantastic redemption stuff. We worked throughout covid while most salons closed but because we collected and dropped properly masked we were not at risk or so they say. Some people's reactions made for hilarious stories. One man opened in door in a full sea divers' outfit and when I got back he paid me with money in a capsule. God I felt like the man form Atlantis. Another customer came to the door in a full monk's habit complete with matching mask. When he paid me in a purse I didn't know whether to thank him or bless him. The older generation, particularly the ladies could not have cared less. "Come in Barry, have a coffee." "I can't," I replied "Restrictions." "Restrictions my arse, sure aren't we dying anyway," was the reply. The most outrageous covid outfit I came across was a lady who answered the door in a beekeeper's regalia, the full lot. When I returned her Bichon that evening she was still in it. She paid me in a honey jar and retreated indoors. I decided to make a friendly quip and said, "See you soon. I'll buzz off now." It fell on deaf ears.

I won't make light of this horrible time. In all our lives, we lost three lovely customers to Covid, two of them with us for years. It's not something I would ever like to live through again. We were lucky to be able to keep going. I can only imagine what it was like for others.

But thankfully we got through it. And thankfully it never entered our house. One of our most elderly customers summed it up for me. One morning as I collected his 18-year-old Cocker Spaniel I asked, "How did you manage Johnny?" "As you know Barry I have lived through a world war and through recessions in the sixties, seventies, and eighties," Johnny replied. "When Covid came I saw hope, people pulling together, helping each other, and just getting back to basics. But now it's nearly gone and all I can see is greed and selfishness returned. Believe me that will kill a lot of people far quicker than Covid or any other disease."

Nail on the head there Johnny.

Chapter 20
Viva Las Vegas

After years of exploring through Africa and Asia we got this buzz to go to Las Vegas. "We have to someday Barry. Why not now? said Collette. "Right," I heartily agreed and off I went and booked the Luxor hotel for ten nights. Ten nights. People looked at me incredulously. Three nights in Las Vegas is enough. A flight to Heathrow from Dublin and then a 2-hour waiting time for the Virgin Atlantic flight to Las Vegas. Everything seemed good. Dublin to Heathrow was no problem, plenty of time as we waited for the flight to come on the departure screen. Collette noticed it wasn't there and I said, "No problem it will appear in a minute." But it never did. "Go and ask them Collette ordered. "Plenty of time. It's an hour away yet," I replied. When it did not appear on the screen I enquired at the desk. The girl at the counter gave me a startled look. "You are in the wrong terminal and that flight leaves in 45 minutes. You need to get over there very quickly."

I nearly dropped. She rang ahead and then got us a buggy to get us over there. It took nearly a half hour as Heathrow is such a big place. Once in the right terminal we got to passport control and had to go through for a second time and the queue was massive. Our dream Las Vegas holiday was disappearing. "Our flight is leaving in five minutes," Collette shouted loudly. "Can we please skip the line?"

Everyone stood to the side and we raced to the top of the line, got through and as we got our bags everyone started clapping and cheering, "go girl go" they urged Collette.

We had five minutes to get to the gate so we had to run and Run we did. At one stage Collette had her shoes in her hand and as we saw the gate our hearts sank. Everyone had already boarded. The Holiday was over before it started. Suddenly a girl appeared in front of us waving frantically. "Come on," she roared. "Hurry up!" Passports checked and she had us on the plane and in our seats in no time. "You are so lucky we were delayed for 15 minutes" she told us, "otherwise the doors were shut and we were gone." The doors shut after us to clapping and cheers again as we flopped back in our seats. The girl who had guided us on-board smiled and said again how lucky we were. I smiled back, thanking her again for her help, as Collette was still in a trance. Doors closed and Las Vegas here we come.

We took Las Vegas by storm after our near disaster, making up for it by taking in everything we could. We kicked off by standing at the viewing point over the Grand Canyon standing on the specially constructed Glass ceiling. You could see right down the Canyon, and we walked gingerly across it hoping it would not crack under the weight of so many people, a both frightening and rewarding experience. A trip to Los Angeles was next, and they showed us everything form the Hollywood sign to Rodeo Drive, Sunset Boulevard, and homes of the stars like Frank, Deano, Michael Jackson, and Lucille Ball and too many more to name.

We saw the Troubadour Club where stars like Elton John, Blondie and the Ramones played toy name but a few. It was fascinating and even included the toilet block where George Michael was arrested, which gave us a strange thrill. At then back late that night across the desert for a large Sloppy Joe sandwich, each of which would give an elephant a heart attack and a beer and off to bed wondering what the next day would bring. Always a fan of live shows a friend of mine had advised me to go down to the ticket office where you could pick up tickets for the top shows for half price or less if you were prepared to wait around. I looked at the billboards showing the acts and prices and right away the temptations jumped out at me, $55 dollars per ticket. I approached the young lady on duty in the booth. A quick computer checks and she raised her head to tell me I could have two tickets for $30. A bargain to see the Motown legends for $30 dollars each I said. "No its £30 for the 2 tickets," she replied. I almost ran back to the hotel and couldn't curb my excitement as I told Collette about my wonderful Coup. Looking suspiciously at both the back and front of the tickets Collette announced it was indeed a result. Temptations here we come.

Out of the hotel at 7pm that evening we grabbed a taxi and off we went for our 8pm show. We gave the taxi driver the address and he said, "you know that's on the north side the strip." "Is that a problem?" we asked. "No," he replied, "not for me it's not." Five minutes later we got to our destination. We paid him and as we walked in he shouted, "Good Luck in there." From the moment we entered the place we knew it was different. Drinks were $2 compared to the $5 we were paying in the Luxor and Meals were priced from $5 down. We showed our tickets and into the show we went, just as it was about to start.

The intro music started, lots of clapping and cheering and then lights up and there we were the only two Caucasians in a sea of Black people. As the temptations broke into "Papa was a rolling stone," the crowd was clapping and swaying like an FA cup final. A Big bosomed lady of rather large proportions waved her hands high and with a large smack of her swinging hips and posterior stung me into life. Likewise for Collette as on her other side she was told, "rise lady this is the Temptations." We danced and swayed for the next two hours at the marvellous show - such a wonderful experience. As we left it seemed like everyone was waving at us and as we waited for a cab I said to the attendant, "wonderful people in there." "Yeah man," he replied "but don't believe it. They just can't get over the fact that two snowflakes turned up to a Temptations show." Home James!

Tom Jones was in town for a residency at the MGM just a few minutes from us. "We have to go," said Collette, a huge fan of the Welsh crooner. "Right," I said and off I went the next morning at 8am to the ticket booth. $150 dollars a ticket was the price on the billboard to see Tom. I took my friends advice and waited a while but at 10am still no sign of a price drop. "Damn I muttered to myself - I might have to cough up $300 for this." I approached the young man at the ticket office and cheekily enquired if that was the best price. "Yes," he said, "it's a weekend show so no chance of that price dropping." I asked was it the same on Saturday and Sunday and he said yes and that the residency was finished on Sunday. Unless he added we could go tonight. "Right" I said, "how much for that?" A little computer work and he gave me a big smile and informed me he could do that night for $25 dollars a ticket each. I got my card out as quick as possible and handed it to him, he wrote down some details swiped the card and the card failed.

"There must be some mistake I said, Can you try again." He tried again but no luck I could not believe it. My card was ok the day before so what was happening. I said try once more. He did and said it wouldn't go through. An impatient crowd was forming behind me trying to get my knockdown Tom Jones tickets. Suddenly he looked at my card and the details he had written down. "Sorry, how do you spell your name?" he asked. "McDonough" I replied at the top of my voice. "Ah" he said, "I have a different spelling." A quick swipe of the card and Bingo the tickets were mine. I could not believe my luck Yippee!

As I went to leave to inform Collette of my master stroke a voice called out from behind me, "excuse me." I turned to find an elderly lady wanting to know if I had just spelt out my name as McDonough. "Yes," I said warily looking around in case it was a scam of some sort to rob my Tom Jones Tickets. "I don't believe it," she said to her companion, obviously her son as he was a lot younger, "Thirty years and at last I found someone who shares my maiden name." Bert did not seem extremely interested. "Can we sit down for just a little while," she asked as I clutched my Tickets close to my chest. I relented and sat. As I did Bert was sent to the Bar about the only thing that seemed to cheer Bert up. Copious amounts of Coors Lite and a few stiff measures of Jack Daniels later and the conversation was flowing. Edith was originally from Mullingar in Westmeath. I was from Meath, so we were geographically very close. She moved to America fifty years ago and had settled in Nevada. She loved Ireland and wanted to know everything that had happened there, and I was happy to oblige. Two hours later Bert as dropping hints about moving on with continuous looks at his watch and fingers drumming on the table. Mum eventually got the hint and after swapping addresses and plenty of hugs and kisses, a handshake from Bert and we parted. Outside the sun was hot and the desert breeze cold and the air hit me like a train. I was locked.

My hotel room was only a 5-minute walk away or it would be if I went the right direction. After 10 minutes I could not recognize anything but managed to figure out I must be going the wrong way and turned around and started in the opposite direction. Twice I walked past the hotel before a young police officer took pity on me and eventually took me to the front door of the Luxor. I headed into the lift and staggered into my room, tickets held triumphantly aloft and related the whole story to Collette, who looked at me in total wonder. I fell onto the bed and as I slowly fell into a slumber I muttered, "it could only happen in Vegas." No Barry," Collette replied, "it could only happen to you."

So sobered up and freshly washed we headed to the MGM hotel for the show that evening. Even at the age of 70, Tom Jones is still one hell of a performer, going through all of his hits over the years. We felt privileged to be part of the 1200 strong audience to witness a magnificent show. And then just before he finished, he told a story a story about growing up in Wales. As he walked past his parents' door his mother would remark "Well look at you, fresh suit, and slicked back hair. Do you think you are Tony Curtis?"

"Well I did," he said, "and actually folks the great man himself is here tonight." The lights turned to the table next to us and there he was, Tony Curtis. He stood up and raised his trademark Stetson hat smiling out of those piercing blue eyes and taking the applause that rang out around the venue. It was one of those surreal moments in life, sitting next to one of Hollywood's greatest stars. This was the man who, as well as starring in many great films, wooed thousands of women including the iconic Marilyn Monroe. As Collette looked on in amazement I pulled her closer and held on to her tightly so she could not escape. He was too close for comfort and I wasn't taking any chances. When we left Las Vegas after our ten nights I felt as though we gave it everything. Aside from the details here we had other great days and nights out. Bette Midler, Barry Manilow, and Vegas' take on Andrew Lloyd Webbers Phantom of the Opera. We renewed our vows in the Little White Chapel - well if its good enough for Elvis it good enough for us. We even got to visit the famous pawn shop in Freemont famous in the television show Pawn Stars. A totally memorable trip that will live with us forever. Crass maybe, Bawdy maybe, Trashy definitely, but nonstop fun day and night. When we got back I met up with my friends who told me three days in Las Vegas was enough. How did I get on, they enquired? "You told me ten days in Las Vegas was too much," I said. "Yes," they said, a look of I told you so on their faces. "Believe me," I said "ten days was not enough!"

Chapter 21
You always remember your first

So many dogs over the years with so many different personalities. But we can still remember back to our first ever dog for Grooming, Donna's Charlie a truculent Westie who always looking smashing after his groom. When Charlie passed, Donna acquired the terrible twins, two little half Yorkshire terriers that were adorable. They stayed with us many times and they were absolutely hilarious fun. Baxter from Ballymum was another who would not give Collette a moments piece. He danced, he snarled, and he snapped but he always got done and went home looking great.

Two days before Christmas some years ago Kevin arrived at the door of the salon with Baxter. Baxter was in pain he said, and the vet couldn't see him. Would we have a look. "We are not vets," I told Kevin, but he begged us. "Please just see if you can do anything," and then belted for the door. "Hold on Kevin," I shouted, "are you not staying?" "No," said Kevin. "He would never forgive me." The problem with Baxter was not serious. A bit of his pooh had stuck to his hair and after several washes and some painstaking plucking he was right as rain again. Kevin came to collect him. Extremely grateful and his sheer look of delight to see his Baxter back to normal again was a delight to see. I'm glad to say Kevin is still with us to this day but poor Baxter has gone to Doggy heaven. Kevin replaced him with another Pomeranian after a while and he has the same temperament that Baxter had, maybe even worse. If there is reincarnation, then this is a true example of it but at least we have the knowledge Baxter lives forever.

Daisy from Duleek was another regular visitor to us. A lovely natured Collie who was a joy to groom. The only exertion that Daisy would put upon herself was to leap onto the grooming table no matter how high. "Groom me," Daisy would say to you. A good wash and Daisy was gone for the afternoon. Sometimes she had to be roused from her Slumber at home time – she sure did love her comfort.

Ted, another Collie was also one to jump on the table hoping to get this inconvenience over as quick as possible. The difference was when grooming was over he would leap form the table straight into the bath before returning to the drying cage for a long snooze before home.

Ross from Bettystown was another favourite of ours. Collected early, he spent a good part of the day with us before returning home in the evening. Not a peep out of Ross the entire day. You could do anything with him. As I left him home of an evening he would saunter out of the van, wander into his owner Martina and before I left would angrily look at me and commence an unmerciful howling as if to tell his owner what an absolute Bastard I was. Ross did this every time I brought him home. We did not see Ross for a while and then when Martina phoned to book him in she told us his eyesight had been getting steadily worse and he was now completely blind and asked if that would be a problem for us. "Not at all," I told her, "we will just guide him."

I collected Ross early as usual, brought him up, lifted him gently and guided him into the salon. Groomed and washed Ross settled down for his customary sleep before home. That evening Martina was delighted as Ross fumbled his way into the house. "How was he Barry?" she enquired. "No different than usual," I told her, "just had to guide him a little as he walks into thing." "Yeah that's what he does here," she replied. She laughed and added, "on the bright side at least he's not squealing on you anymore." I tuned to go when Ross appeared at the front door. Looking at me he unleashed a loud guttural whine and looked up at Martina who burst out laughing. Ross may be blind as a bat but he was still ratting me out.

Yorkies are adorable and we have loads of them, all with different characters. Spike and Busty from Drogheda, belonging to Gemma were among our first ever. Sadly, they are no longer with us but after time Gemma got another pair Max and Bailey who were just as adorable.

Pebbles from Finglas was another character. A great man for the Ladies was Pebbles. Maddy from Bettystown was a beautiful specimen of the breed alongside our own two teacup from Ratoath, another fine example of this beautiful breed of dog. Then there is Bosco who stayed with us for a while and a right livewire he was and probably our oldest surviving yorkie, Alfie from Curragha. A real pleasure to groom he is and though we have been doing it for years he looks no different than he did when he first came to us. I say to his owner that I think she's using Botox on him.

Then there is Izzy. Izzie's owner asked us to mind him for a few weeks as her house was being renovated. He ended up staying 2 months and a nicer and funnier house guest you could not meet. She warned me that Izzy was not a great eater and she was right. For the first few days he just nibbled at his food and so we introduced Izzy to ham. And by God did Izzy take to it. He just loved it. In the evening Collette used to give our new Pomeranian Puppy Gaga a ham treat. Izzy seeing this ran from her bed and would literally Jump 5 foot off the floor to try snatch it from Collette's hand. Gaga would try to match her and it was a hilarious sight to watch the two of them trying to outjump each other every evening. Izzy always came out on top. Within a week Izzy was eating like a baby Labrador and the fun she brought to all including Gaga was heart-warming. Izzy was an out and out character.

King Charles dogs were plentiful too in the salon. A lovely placid breed of dog and so faithful to their owners. Maggie form Garristown was a regular visitor. A smashing looking dog that always when home looking perfect. Unfortunately, Maggie passed on, but her owner Hilary got another lovely King Charles called Ruby and to this day we still have her, and she too always look perfect after her groom. A beautiful animal.

Molly is probably the oldest King Charles we have, blind now but still coming to us after a lot of years and thankfully still fighting fit. Toby who lives around the corner from us is a bigger size of the breed, but a strikingly handsome dog. He comes reluctantly, behave impeccably once here, and goes home looking like a King Charles should look. A well-groomed King Charles is a sight to behold!

Westies were once our most popular breed that came for grooming. Over the years though the number of westies has declined rapidly. It's a pity really, as some of the Westies we had coming gave us some great memories. Orla's two in Laytown were a great example. They always came together - just as well really, as if apart for two minutes they would wail like banshees until reunited. Collected together, washed together, groomed together on the table and then home together. When one of them died, we didn't think the other one would last long. He did though. Luckily, Orla's mums Shih Tzu was being rehomed at her house and this kept him going for a good spell longer. Westies are a lot tougher than they look.

Today we only have a few westies that come in, Lucy around the corner and one in Laytown. They are beginning to look like a dying breed what with all the new breeds coming through and this is a real pity. As tough as they are, we will always remember the affection that they gave us, even old Dirty Harry whom I mentioned earlier who at times ran us ragged. Like his owner Eileen we shed a tear at his passing too. Bichons are still plentiful despite the introduction of all these new breeds and we still have some of the old brigade left. Our electrician Shane would regularly be called upon to fix something in the salon and I return Bert and Ernie grooming free. Barter at its best.

Bert and Ernie came to us for years and a good old shindig would they give Collette. Both were like old friends, and they were coming that long that we were really shocked to hear recently that Bert had died. Once again it struck me that Ernie would not last long without him but last he did. He's still here and if the last visit he had with us is anything to go by he's not going anywhere yet.

Unlike the Westies Bucshon's still seem to be a popular breed. Lucy, Sake, and Kia are all regulars with us and the Maltese Bobby who we mind quite regularly is another great visitor. I love Bobby. The way he interacts with other dogs is so engaging. He's a pocket rocket, barrel of fun and all our dog love Bobby to bits especially Impala. When bobby arrives he behaves exactly as he does in his own house and never frets. He just simply adapts and is pure heaven to have. It's his attitude to life I love with Bobby. It's a case of "wherever I lay my hat…" still.

Chapter 22
Out with the old and in with the new

The canine world is changing as I have already said, and the older dog breeds seem to be fading out and a lot of new ones coming in. Labradoodles, Cock-a-poos, French Bulldogs, and others whose names I cannot even pronounce. The times certainly are a changing.

I began to wonder if the likes of the dear old Labrador or the ever-pleasant springer spaniel were going to disappear forever. Thank god it didn't happen and our quota of the older breeds stayed steady and after a while even increased. Only the demise of the dear old Westie seems prevalent.

Now the Cock-a-poo is a lovely looking dog but a lot of people seem to forget they need very regular brushing otherwise they matt and matt very badly. I am not a dog groomer but I do know from being around dogs a long time that if they don't get the attention they need their coat will deteriorate badly. Leaving any groomer with no option but to shave the coat to relieve the dog's discomfort. When I say Brush I mean a deep brush, not just the top of the coat but deep down, otherwise you are wasting your time. Some people point to the fact that the dogs coat is fluffy. Well yes it is but only on the top. Underneath matts have formed which could lead to skin problems. Just a bit off, I've heard said. I want him fluffy and looking nice. It does not work like that I'm afraid. The only option for a badly matted dog is to shave it and some people just don't get that. That said a lot of responsible dog owners do understand and thankfully we have lots of good dog owners. "Do whatever you have to do," is a common saying to us. Whatever is best for the dog. It's difficult to tell the owner that their dog has no choice but to be shaved and it does not make you popular, but I'm afraid that is the reality of it and not just for Cock-a-poo breeds. For some reason, their hair seems to matt more quickly and particularly in wet weather. So the advice is simple. Brush or comb regularly and not just the topcoat. Get right down. Remember if you don't Brush Brushy, Collette will have to Shavy Shavy.

Chapter 23
The perfect pair

Around the corner from us lives Ger who owns two greyhounds. You can set your clock most days by Ger who walks them every morning at the same time. Two beautiful soft-hearted creatures that we have had the pleasure of grooming and minding over the years, Greyhounds are lazy, the original couch potatoes. They hate the cold, love heat, and adore sleep. They love plenty of human contact and no problem with that at the salon. Even if the cage drier is not on them and on another dog the heat it generates would have them asleep in minutes. Both love to watch the busy activity that goes on in the salon without having any great desire to participate in any way. Both dogs love the sun on their backs and on a hot day both stretch out lovingly lapping up the rays with the only movement visible being the odd tail wag.

They do need to be walked every day, not a chore really given the leisurely pace at which both dogs walk and they seem to have perfected walking in tandem. Not even the sight of a stray Tabby cat could stir these two into action. At home where both dogs spend their very limited outdoor time during the winter, we have two kennels to protect the dos from rain or showers. Each kennel would hose a medium to large dog in case of a sudden cloud burst and they can shelter there until it passes.

On one such day as we were in the salon a sudden April shower came and a heavy downpour it was too. On looking out the window we saw that one kennel was empty while the other one had two pairs of legs and two tails sticking out of it. Somehow the pair of them had managed to squeeze in together. I went out to check and they were wrapped around each other like one of Picasso's weird paintings that you see in Rome. I could make out two grinning heads, so I left them until the shower passed. And when it did, they emerged, untangled, and stretched like a pair of Yoga teachers. It was hilarious to watch the devotion these two creatures had for each other and also heartwarming. They bring joy every time they stay with us, long may it continue.

Flossie the lovely Lurcher was coming to stay for Christmas. Lyn, whose husband was from Portugal had arranged a visit to his hometown for Christmas, so long as we could look after Flossie. "No problem," we told Lyn, "we are here anyway." And Flossie was an absolute dote. Lyn was an avid walker and I had passed her many times as she flew down the road with Flossie trotting beside her, so I told Lyn I could not guarantee Flossie would get a workout at the same pace as she gave her. "Don't worry," said Lyn, "she won't complain – that I can assure you." Flossie is an absolute darling and over Christmas we got plenty of opportunity to walk her, but Flossie was basically not that interested in her walks. One afternoon however as we were walking in Ashbourne we passed my local "The Stag's Head." A sudden loud roar spilled out of the pub window, the door banged open and Tom a friend of mine emerged with a huge smile on his face. "Alright Baz!" he shouted. "United have just gone 1 up." Flossie dragged me through the front door of the pub and stared straight up at the television showing the game live. She sat on all fours, transfixed by the TV. "Of course," I said to myself, Lynn is a massive Manchester United fan so this is normal for Flossie. When the game was over and United had won I swear Flossie was smiling. There was plenty of good-natured banter over my sudden appearance with Flossie from the regulars and plenty of attention for the lady herself. Off home we went, Flossie with a new spring in her step.

On our return Flossie ate heartily and seemed far more content with herself. Over the next few days Flossie would always stop outside the Stags head as we passed but only once more did she catch a united game. And once again it was the same story- she sat on all floors transfixed by the TV and when United won again, she seemed to perk up dramatically. This time she nearly dragged me home! That night I tried to work out what part of the theory Flossie fell into. Most dogs that stay with us are given a toy of some sort or maybe a plastic bone or even their own bed from home. Not Flossie- she wanted to watch Man United. But why?

Was it because she thought Lyn was closer while watching the game, or it felt familiar or was it just that Man United had won. Whatever the case it did not really matter, Flossie slept with a smile on her face. The next day while dropping Flossie home, I ran my thoughts by Lyn. "Yeah," Lyn said, "Loves United does Flossie, but you were very lucky Barry." "Whys that," I asked her. "Well if you had made her watch Liverpool she would never talk to you again!

Chapter 24
Santa's Deer Dogs

Years ago Samoyeds were a regular feature of our days' work but over the years they seem to have decreased in popularity. I can't explain why because they really are beautiful animals. Nowadays we only have two, but what beautiful specimens of the breed they are.

Dasher and Kodie are regular visitors to us both for grooming and minding. Beautiful looking and with marvellous temperaments they were an absolute joy to both of us even if they were lots of work, when you see them snow white and resplendent as they leave to go home. They would literally lick you to death as you spent hours de-matting and drying these marvellous creatures. Every December they would have to come in on a certain date to get ready for the job they were born for which was pulling a sleigh through the village of Ratoath. It was a magnificent sight to watch these two gleaming white beauties tromp happily along with their sleigh of presents sliding behind them as children looked on at this wondrous sight.

They also stayed with us throughout the year and never a dull moment. A walk with these two was not a walk on the wild side. During the winter months when they stayed and I brought them out in the frost I must have resembled a scene from "Alaska - the final frontier," as people cheerfully waved and bid me good morning as I slid past them.

But for dogs meant for the outdoors, these two had other ideas. As soon as temperatures dropped, two fluffy heads appeared at the window of the salon, yelping for comfort. And once inside, forget about leaving their warm comfy beds. This pair had it sussed. Dash had developed for a fetish for plastic over the years and the first mistake I made was to feed them in plastic bowls. Kodie ate the food. Dasher did too and then decided to eat the two bowls as well. I could hear a commotion outside the salon window and there he was, plastic everywhere and him happily smiling at me with his Joker faced impish grin.

Another time when bringing them in one evening I got distracted for five minutes and left them in the garden area. They were perfectly safe there, but the garden hose wasn't! It took him just that length of time to dismantle it. As I went to get them, there he was surrounded by lots of yellow plastic hose bits, grinning at me like a Cheshire cat. Kodie had no interest in such childishness - she just wanted to get to her bed.

We had gotten matts from Christie's suppliers for the kennels that no dog would ever tear or scratch, or so we were told, But no-one told Dash that. One night on the mat and the next morning it was ripped to shreds, his big happy grin saying, "What do you think about that!" "What do I think of that," I yelped at Dash, "I think it's just as well I love you; you menace." He never stopped grinning. Kodie looked at me as if to say, "baby it's cold outside," Ant and Dec my backside - no match for Kodie and Dash.

Two Glistening Snow Dogs

Chapter 25
Adiós mi amigo Binx

"Barry I need a favour," Noel asked me in the Stags Head over a pint. "Sure Noel, I will collect Binx in the morning," I said. "Yes I want him groomed," Noel replied, "but I also need you to bring him to the Airport on Monday." I looked at Noel wide eyed for a minute and then I twigged. Noel was bringing Binx on holidays. "Ah Noel, I joked, "What's wrong, can you not bear to be parted with him for a few weeks." "No Barry," Noel replied, "We are going for good." I nearly dropped. Noel was a loyal customer for years and Binx was a beautiful Shi Tzu we had been grooming for years. "But are you sure," I said, "Big decision and all that." "No, we go on Saturday Barry and Binx is booked for Monday. Can you do it?" I asked, "What about family Noel, will no one bring him up for you." "Has to be you," said Noel, "I couldn't trust anybody else. Better he sees you before he gets on the plane." I agreed to do it and Noel was happy

It was a difference job to my usual routine, but it was what Noel wanted and that's what counted. Next morning Binx was collected, and Noel gave me all the necessary papers for Monday. He was heading off Monday at 11 o'clock. Binx was his usual happy self in the salon no idea what was in front of him, and Collette made a huge fuss of him. As we left to go back to Noels daughters house, I suspected I saw a few tears. Monday morning I collected Binx from

Noel's daughter and made for Dublin airport about 20 minutes away. Safely ensconced in his cage Binx was beside me in the van looking a little confused, he knew that this was not normal. As we entered the airport the plane seemed to frighten him, as he cowered in the back of the cage.

I drove to the holding area where Binx was to go and got out with Binx' cage in my hands, waiting for someone to see me. A young girl appeared and just took my documents, "all in order," she said as she reached for the cage. Poor Binx froze. He looked at me in total alarm "Don't hand me over," his look said, "it's alright Binx," I started to say, "Daddy's at the other side. Two hours and lots of Sunny weather, Paella, and sexy Spanish dogs. They even have win-a-lot over there and lovely beaches for you to run up and down" I was beginning to ramble so I shut up which was just as well as Binx was looking at me as if I was mad. The attendance looked and incredulously as I gave things a final wave "I'm not convinced he bought all that," I said to her. She replied, "well he should have because I sure did." She gave me a flashing smile and I felt better. Binx was going to be ok.

I got a text from Noel that night. Thanks a million, it said. El Binx has landed and he's great by the way did you check that message I left in the envelope. I suddenly remembered the girl handing me back the envelope saying something wasn't part of Binx papers. I went to my coat and checked it. It simply said 2.30pm, Chepstow on Tuesday "it's a new life." A keen gambler Noel, I think he was giving me one last hurrah. I put a tenner on it the next morning just for old times' sake and it romped home at 15 to 1. €150 won. I could not believe it but as I collected my winnings that evening I smiled broadly as the girl counted out my money. I looked at the sky and out loud said

"Thanks Binx." Who is Binx?" the girl asked. "Just a dog I put on a plane to Spain," I replied. She looked at me stunned. I left laughing.

Goodbye Mister Binx

Chapter 26
It's a Doggy neighbourhood

We have been operating along our road for nearly sixteen years now, dogs coming and going sometimes late at night and sometimes early in the morning but without the understanding of our neighbours it would have been impossible to run this business. We are incredibly lucky that not only do they understand what we try to do, they support us whenever they can. I feel I must mention them for all the goodwill they have shown us.

At the end of the road lives Rocky a real character who is probably one of our oldest customers. A striking Bichon, he always looks magnificent when groomed and is adored by owner Janice and by us too - an absolute treasure.

Across the road form Rocky is Benji. It took a lot of grooming sessions to get Benji on side but finally we have won him round and I think he enjoys coming to us now - not that Benji would admit that! His owner Caroline brought him elsewhere to get groomed years ago because Benji was having none of it and we are not equipped like a vet is to deal with difficult dogs. But when she asked if we would like to try him again, we agreed and Collette won him over. He is now established as one of our favourites just don't tell Benji that.

Up from Benji are Noel and Isabella with their beautiful Yorkie Bella a real picture of a teacup yorkie – tough on the outside but a real angel in the salon. Whenever she sees me outside the salon she barks like crazy as she always thinks I'm coming for her. Isabella's sister has a cracking King Charles who always comes up with Bella for grooming. They tell us they don't really get on at home, but they should see them in the saloon - doghouse devils become salon angels. Both go home picture perfect.

Or it's Jack Russell has finally given in to us. Difficult at the start, he seems to have accepted his faith now and even seems to enjoy his drying period. Even so, as soon as he sees me through the window coming to collect him, he scarpers and hides - a real character.

Caroline's Archie frequented us for years, a big shaggy Himalayan breed who love his grooming session. He was a lot of work our Archie but it was worth to see him resplendent as he went home. Sometimes I would collect Archie if no one was home and he was always looking up at the sky. Even when it rained Archie just sat there on all fours staring above - even heavy snow would not deter him. He's just sat there.

"He won't come inside" Caroline told me. "No matter what we try. He has his bed inside but he just wants to be out all the time no matter what the weather. I think good weather bores him, he just loves the rain, the heavier the better for old Archie."

We minded Archie on a few occasions and she was spot on. Archie was an outdoor dog and at evening time as it got cooler we had to entice Archie in with treats. He would settle for the night, but early next morning he would nearly break the door down to get out and then would assume his sitting position gazing at the sky. Archie was waiting for rain. When Archie passed, Loki arrived in Caroline's. A stunning Labradoodle, jet black in colour and not for Loki great outdoors. Oh No! Loki wasn't going out he wanted his comfort. Loki stayed with us as well and one drop of rain and he would whine to get in. A warm bed and a nice sprinkling of other dogs to converse with was much more Loki's style.

Buzz, an energetic and lovable Cocker spaniel is another frequent guest with us. When Buzz was returning home after his stay I would tell him that morning "Well Buzz, mammy's coming home today." Buzz would spend the day galloping around the garden trying to look over the walls to see where mammy was. When they did arrive Buzz would dance with delight before bolting into the back seat, giving us that big Buzz grin before departing. Buzz loved his dental sticks. Sometimes I would have one in my mouth to tease him. Buzz would whip it out of my mouth and sit there for a while as if smoking it. What a sight that was - a Cocker spaniel having a drag of a dental stick cigar while grinning cheekily at you. Buzz was the Del Boy of the canine world and by God he knew it.

There have been so many good neighbours and customers over the years that have supported us a lot of them even becoming our friends. It takes a lot to trust your dog with somebody when it's part of your family or as one customer remarked me one day "I'm giving my dog to a man in a van to bring to a lady with a scissors and she always comes home happy" and that sums it up for me. We do appreciate all these people and believe me there are a lot more that I haven't mentioned but certainly haven't forgotten. We have never really thanked them all either - until now.

Chapter 27
Sammy - The Persian Player

"I'd like a cat," announced Collette. After years of puppy licks and waggy tails she wanted a loving companion to snuggle up to in the evening time when our troops had crashed out. A kitty, a white Persian one, all fluffy and cuddly." "Right," I said, "leave it to me." Famous last words and so off I went in search of feline beauty. Persian cats were not easy to find in Southern Ireland so I headed north to Enniskillen to a breeder whose ad stated that you would not go home without one of the litter. On arrival at the large stone house in the countryside surrounded by superb gardens I was welcomed inside by a woman and there seemed to be cats everywhere - on the large stage stairs, they prowled like tigers, eyeing me with great suspicion. Into a room at the back of the house and she proudly pointed to a new litter of pure-bred Persians. They were Persians alright - ginger Persians. "They are not White," I said "No," she said, "not fully white half white half ginger." Those cats are brown I cried. "No," she retorted "just not fully white." On top of that they were huge. They are huge I almost yelled. "Oh well" she said, "they had a big mommy and daddy."

I did not know what to think and as I was about to leave one of them came over to me and started to rub himself seductively against my hand. "Look," she said, "he likes you." He might well have done but

I said to her, "I don't think it's what I'm looking for - I was looking for something a lot smaller." "But it's only a Kitten," she said. "A kitten?" I said, "some of the dogs we groom are smaller than him." "Look," she said, "I'll knock a £100 off if that's what you're after." "That's not the point," I stated. "I drove two hours to get a white Persian kitten and you want me to go home with cheetah." I flourished the ad to her, reading aloud what it said. "Well my sister deals with the advertisement part of things," she said. The ginger Jones looked up at me as if to say don't leave me here mate. Bring me home and I'll make it worth your while." "Right," she said, "another £50 for petrol," and the cat was now £350 and emotional extortion was also being used. "No," I said to myself. I must stand firm. Yeah Right! An hour later I was driving through Ardee with Garfield in the back. And then we got home.

Collette looked at this giant kitten as it peered out of the cage. He's not White," she exclaimed in anguish. "Not fully," I said. "Not at all," she said. I could not argue. "He's not a kitten," she declared. "big mummy and daddy I mumbled stupidly. "Who was the daddy Clarence the cross-eyed Lion?" she replied referring to the series in the 70s Called Daktari. He is a Persian I said, clearly on the defensive. She looked at him and then said "Well, one out of three is something I suppose."

Carrier doors open out the kitten came, striding majestically across the couch. Our two boys loved him and were busy stroking him and Collette eventually gave in. As he ambled over to her she started to stroke him. But as I gave a sigh of relief he turned and looked at me and in the eyes he gazed intently from was one word: Sucker!. Sammy the cat was home. From the moment Sami arrived he let it be known that this was his joint, majestically striding around the house from bedroom to bedroom, along the stairs and into the kitchen to view what delights were going to feed him. If not the best of treats Sammy would not touch and meowed constantly until he got what he wanted. When he ventured outside it was only to wreck the dog's head. Posing on the wall tops driving them nuts, Sammy knew they could not get near him and sometimes I'd swear he was laughing at them.

After a year and fully grown as if he wasn't huge already, Sammy reckoned on investigating outside the front of the house. Sitting on the front wall Sammy would view the children heading to school at 9 o'clock every morning. They would stop in dozens to stroke him and they all knew him by name. At three he would see them again going home when it was the same scenario. Plenty of "hello Sammy's" followed by another stroke or two. Sammy would reward them with a Royal Miaow. We all reckoned what a lovely friendly character but Sammy was not just being social - Sammy was weighing up the street. It was not just a home he wanted – it was the whole street.

Across the road from us lived Tony, a likeable eccentric who also had a cat. One morning as I went off early to Blanchardstown, I spotted Sammy going in his window. I waited for him to be evicted but with no sign I drove off. When I returned two hours later Sammy was coming out of Tony's window obviously well fed and happy. I asked Tony that afternoon if Sammy was annoying him. "Not at all," said Tony, "he drops in for a quick bite, settles himself with my cat Socks for a bit of a chat and then off he goes. He's a beautiful cat Barry," Tony said, "he's always welcome here."

Next door to Tony lived Anne who also had a cat and Tony told me later that Sammy was also a regular visitor there. "Yes Barry when my food is not to his liking he jumps over the wall and dines there. I think he gets tuna and chicken in that establishment. I can't compete with that I'm afraid." Dogs are loyal creatures' cats are not. They are not loyal, and they will cheat to get anything they want in the feline world Sammy was Maradona.

On a spring morning I left Ashbourne to go to Laytown to collect Zadie Wogan a regular with us for years. As I pulled out I glanced to my right and there was Sammy stretched over the top of Anne's couch, enjoying the morning sunshine, and getting ready for the day ahead. He raised his right paw as if to wave at me and then he smirked as I drove off. When I came back I saw him coming out of Tony's who informed me later that Anne was not up to give him his breakfast. She was obviously up that evening because when I came back from Laytown, there he was again lying on the back of the couch looking out quite content. I went inside to inform Collette and the boys that Sammy had moved out what an ungrateful wretch he was all three of them just laughed heartily. To them it was funny, to me betrayal. Sammy didn't give a damn either way. Sammy stayed there for eight months smirking at me every time I went past and when Anne moved in with her daughter Sammy arrived in the front door looked at his empty bowl disgustedly and ambled upstairs to Clintons room. He curled up on the bed – the prodigal cat had returned but there was no tail between his legs.

One summer evening I heard Paul next door playing music outside. Paul had grand taste in music and I always cocked an ear to what he was playing. I heard him talking to what I assumed was one of his sons trying to educate them to the music of the 70s and 80s "Listen to this guy here," I heard Paul say. "Listen to the base it's just brilliant." It was if I recall a Springsteen number. When it finished Paul said in a loud voice "What do you think Sammy - is it good or what?" I could not resist a peek over the fence and sure enough there

Paul, playing his music and Sammy sat in rapt attention. There was nowhere that this cat won't get too.

As we ate our dinner one afternoon Clinton dropped his knife and fork and sat transfixed staring out the front window. Collette stared too, looking shocked. With a shriek of disbelief she managed to utter "Sammy has fallen out the bedroom window. He's dead." We rushed outside to view the remains of our beloved two-faced cat, but he was not there, nothing! "Are you sure it was him?" I queried the same "Barry," she said, "it was a large orange helicopter, tail swirling, legs flaying." Clinton was still in shock, and he just nodded in agreement with his mam. It sure was Sammy alright and as usual he landed on his feet. Sammy breezed in the front door, none the worse for wear and headed to his bowl for a quick snack before he headed up to Clinton's room for a sleep. If a cat really has nine lives Sammy has just used up six of them.

Sammy in his older years had taken to sitting on the grass of the corner of the street, so he could receive even more attention. Everyone knew Sammy and even the parents of the school-going children were now paying homage to him.

One particular day in the summer I left the house to collect a dog and Sammy was in his usual spot. When I arrived back two hours later he was still there taking in the morning sun as he went to bring the dogs back two hours later, he was still there. I stopped and went over to him but he never moved. Sammy always moved. As I lifted him he let out an agonised Miaow. Straight to the vet with him, who informed us that Sammy had broken his femur bone. It was to be painkillers and six weeks rest for Sammy. We stationed him on the living room new bed and every treat available to a cat was given. And Oh My God did he milk it. If Sammy was in need of anything a floor miaow had everybody racing to his needs. Sammy was loving it. After six weeks Sammy was back to his usual self, but I suspect he was right after three - he just knew how to work it.

In his later years Sammy spent a lot of time in Clintons room sitting by his side looking at the computer for a little while before returning to his bed for a curl up and a sleep. They both adored each other. Sammy passed after a short illness and we all missed our mysterious selfish two-faced cat. He was cremated and put up with our other deceased dogs as well but the house still felt quiet - almost eerie. In my converted man cave in the house is where all our animals rest in peace and as I watched the late-Night Football game and was about to head to bed when I heard a loud lingering Miaow. Plenty of cats on our road I thought maybe that's one of them. As I turned the light off the miaow went again. I turned the light on again to check the TV was off, thinking maybe too many cans of cider. Or maybe just maybe Sammy was letting me know that this time he was home to stay. Rest in Peace Sammy.

Sammy the two faced Cat

Chapter 28
Away with Frances Brennan

"I want to go away with Frances Brennan" announced Collette. "What?" I said stunned, "yes," she said. Having just watched a repeat of one of his tour shows, she had decided that she wanted to go from the next one. "Well," I said after some thought, "so does this half the country." "Well I want to go," she said like a child demanding a visit to a fun fair.

In the evening as I read the paper I noticed a small column inviting applicants for interviews for the coming show - it jumped out at me. I showed it to Collette and she was straight onto her phone. Minutes later smiling she said the application was lodged. A week later she received a message requesting her to turn up at a Dublin hotel for an interview. "Good for you," I said. "No," she replied, "good for us you're coming too." Never a great fan of Francis I wondered where I came into it but the following week in the middle of a snowdrift we turned up at the appointed time. "We'll have to wait for a good while," Collette said, "there's bound to be hundreds here," but the weather conditions must have delayed a lot of people because there were only two people in front of us and within fifteen minutes we were in front of the researchers. Five minutes into the very relaxed interview we had them in tears of laughter. They seemed to really love, "Our Lady and the Tramp," scenario and as we left, they told us they would be in touch within a couple of weeks but that we should stay positive. Outside the hotel I said, "That's it, we're in." "What?" exclaimed Collette, "Yep," I exclaimed in total confidence, "piece of cake they loved us. Let's go home and pack our bags." She looked at me a little funny but didn't really argue against my cocky quips, which made me even more sure of our place on the plane. Three weeks passed and we heard nothing. Ever practical Collette said, "Ah well, WE gave it our best shot. Nothing ventured…." "Never say never," I answered, but I must admit my confidence was diminishing. A week later and we both reckoned it was all over - the fat lady had sung.

On a cold April morning I set off for Drogheda to book us a couple of weeks in Turkey. My phone rings and a girl from the production team asked me if we are still OK for the tour the 2nd of May. "But we haven't heard anything," I blustered out. "Well you are now," she replied. "Is this official?" I asked her, "because right now I'm on my way to book two weeks holiday in Turkey." "Well," she said, "I don't have the authority to tell you for sure as there has to be a video link with Janine later but that's really only a formality." "Yes or No," I demanded and a slight paused ensued followed by a whispered, "you're in."

I rang Collette and she had already been called. "It's not for sure," she said. "It is," I said. "She never said that to me," Collette replied. "I threatened her," I said. "With what?" exclaimed Collette. "Two weeks in Turkey!" I turned around and went straight back home and an hour later they did the video link collection with Collette and I on the couch, her lounging like Heidi Klum, me looking like an extra for The Sopranos, they love it. Laughing loudly Janine asked us finally if we were to describe ourselves as dogs what sort would we be. "A poodle" said Collette demurely. "A Rottweiler," said I and let out a loud wail. Laughing again Janine said she looked forward to seeing us both. I turned to Collette "Well, you are going on holidays with Francis Brennan and I'm coming with you." The next three weeks flew by with getting doctors clearance certs and another member of the production crew came to the house to film footage. There were lots of things to be organised but the biggest obstacle seemed to be what clothes to bring and the reason? We had no idea where we were going.

Everywhere went through our heads South America, China, Japan, India, Australia, Sri Lanka or maybe New Zealand - we really had not got a clue. We ruled out Europe but everywhere else in the world must have gone through our heads. "Anyway we won't find out until the morning we're leaving so I'm afraid it's a case of pack and hope," we said.

As we went about our business, people would ask where Francis was bringing us. We couldn't answer them because we hadn't a clue ourselves. We could not verify our bank cards at our local EBS because we did not know where we were headed. Deirdre, behind the counter told us as soon as you find out, you can clear them at the airport. "It will only take a few minutes." "Fne," we said and as we went to go out Deidre said by the way. We turned back to the desk only for her to utter, "make sure you go to the toilet," as she laughed – repeating a famous Francis quip. Everyone seemed to have caught the buzz, the excitement was growing. May 3rd dawned and off to the airport to our appointed meeting place we went and sat waiting to be found. Half an hour later they brought us downstairs, cameras rolling. Francis smiled as we approached him. "Ah, Barry and Collette," he exclaimed, "our dog groomers from Ashbourne. How are you?" "Any idea where we're off to?" said Francis as he waved the national flag of the country we were on our way to. "Brazil," I said hoping I was right. "Not at all," he said and waved his flag again. "It's South Africa." "God Barry," he said, "I thought you would have known, you two having been there before." "Yeah we were," I replied, "and the only thing I cell was a dead rhino." He laughed and we departed and joined the rest of our travelling companions. South Africa here we come.

An 18-hour flight, punctuated by a two hour stop in Dubai lay ahead of us. A long haul but personally I loved it. Flying was always a joy for me. I find it relaxing and the longer the better; plus the thoughts of what waited for us on the other side was tantalising. In Dubai during our stop-over we went into the Emirates priority lounge. About 1/4 of a mile of different foods from throughout the world, Moet champagne and any drink you could think of was laid out before us, all on the house. Needless to say, we took full advantage and I floated onto the plane. We landed on time at Johannesburg, flew through customs made our way to our bus. As we did so we were instructed by the production team to look eager. Well a few of our travel companions did that alright. In their desire to get their faces on camera, they nearly ran anyone in front of them over. Well, I thought, we are only here an hour and already we can identify the Stars in your eye's contestants. Off we went to a small tribal village outside Johannesburg. "It's just like Bunratty," Francis told us, "it's geared for the tourists." After a welcome dance we were shown to our quarters for the night. load on straw hooks outside inside a luxurious bath satellite TV, a mini-bar, and a lovely hot shower. All this in the middle of nowhere. A pre-prepared lunch of zebra, crocodile stew and wildebeest with a few spuds was followed by a spot of spear throwing and then a light supper of toasted crickets and meal worms in front of an open fire. Francis and Collette tried them, while the rest of us bottled it. Never was a bed so welcome as it was that night.

The next day was a walking trip around Johannesburg surrounded by heavy security I'm down to the apartheid museum. The cameras rolled the whole time as we crossed the previous page. At all times, the African security team never took their eyes off us and it looked as though they had even employed some of the local mafia to ensure our safety. A magnificent hotel awaited us that night, the best the city had to offer. The rooms were unbelievable as was the Hollywood type stairs and the magnificent lighting on display throughout. What a pity we had to be up at 5am for a flight to Port Elizabeth, but hey that showbiz folks.

From then on the filming was intense. It just takes, retakes, stand here and say this and began to feel like work, but the fringe benefits were some of the most amazing sights one would ever see, including a safari in one of the most famous parks in the world call Sibuyan. We had to get to it by boat and for thirty hours we were cut off from the world.

Amazing is the only word to describe this safari. A trip to see the elephants one of them looked as if he was going to charge a Jeep until placated by our trusty guide, an evening cocktail as the sun set and back to base camp afterwards. An evening meal around a marvellous open fire as we listened to Francis regale us with stories of his RTE experiences; before retiring to our tents. Tents which contained every luxury one could wish for, lying back contentedly as the roar of the rhino echoed through the night amid the cry of 1000 different birds. At dawn you would see giraffe, elephants, wildebeest, and

Rhinos all share the same water hole. We were sure in Born Free territory. As I have said, it was amazing. A superb breakfast of honey bacon and sausages, fresh coffee and fresh bread and we were on the road again. Over the next few days we witnessed everything that's South Africa had to offer. From Bungee jumping from the world's highest point to eating oysters in the ocean. We got to Soweto and I got to see where Nelson Mandela was born and lived. Just up the road was Bishop Tutu's house, personally the highlight of my tour. I found out later from our guide that they had closed the streets off because it was a TV show. They allowed it he informed me because they wanted to show South Africa in a new life. In the winelands, we drank some of the best wines in the world which we mixed with chocolate that they gave us. When I was doing my personal interview later that day, I informed our producers that when I got home I was off down to Aldi for a bottle of white and a 4-pack of snickers. The Producer had to retake the clip twice as he doubled up laughing alongside the camera man Dave.

Another highlight of the tour was walking with the cheetahs and Collette was chosen for this. With Francis and two others, she walked for an hour with some of the most fearsome creatures on earth. Collette exclaimed later that this was one of the most exhilarating and frightening experiences of her life. Amidst all of this, we even got to visit Ronnie's sex shop in the middle of nowhere, with thousands of bras and knickers hanging from the ceiling. Francis gave Collette a pair of pink ones to add to his collection with Ronnie smiling approvingly as she did. Then we were off to Cape Town for the final leg of the tour. We would spend four days there and could at last unpack suitcases leaving them that way until we were going home.

We got to the hotel at around noon and we're given a drinks reception and quickly booked into our rooms. This was quickly followed by an exodus of our party to Cape Town centre. They stressed they were in need of hairdressers and beauty salons. Well I won't argue with that one. The hotel was quiet after they had all gone. Collette yawned and said, "A hot bath, a nice meal and that's me for the night. I must admit Collette's stamina on this trip has stunned me. For someone who loves the bed more than Casanova she had really kept going.

Fish and chips arrived with a beer for me, and we were in heaven. "Pure heaven," we said, "peace and nowhere to go," as we stretched out contentedly. "Are you not going into town," yelled a voice behind us. We looked around in shock, it was Francis. "No," said Collette, "its bed for me Francis."

"They're all gone to smarten themselves up for the next few days," said Francis, "but sure you don't really need to Collette, do you." I grinned mysteriously to myself. "Anyway I'll join you," said Francis. "Surely to God you are sick looking at all of us by now," I said. "Not at all Barry," he said. We chatted for an hour and a half before bed with him learning a lot about us and us learning a lot about him. It was like, "I'm not in the show here. I can say what I want." A gentleman and a funny one at that he again enquired as to why we had not gone to town. "Collette has a sore throat," I said. "Strepsils," replied Francis, "they are the best. "Yeah," I replied, "I'm going to try find some now." "No need," and he was gone. Ten minutes later he was back, a packet of Strepsils in hand. "Here you go Collette," he said. Get a few of them into you and you will be fine." And she was though I'm not sure if it was the Strepsils themselves or Francis showing he cared! Collette was knackered. Eleven days of constant movement was getting to her. She required sleep while I had to be out for a few hours every evening otherwise I was up at cock crow. As Collette slept I went to the lobby bar and teamed up with the south African security team who were looking after us. Lovely guys that I had some crack with for an hour or two. Sometimes Finbarr, a lovely gentleman from Cork would join us and maybe a production crew member or two. Like me, Finbarr was not part of the clique that had formed among our fellow travellers. The days in Cape Town were marvellous, a trip to Table Mountains rewarding us with fabulous views. True Heaven on earth.

We made a trip to an Ostrich farm, where Francis informed Collette that Ostrich feather dusters were among the best cleaning devices he had ever used and that she really had to invest in some. "How would I get them home," she asked. He had a long tubular case Francis told her and that they could go in with his, no problem at all. So off she went to a shanty town outside Cape Town. This was a marvellous insight into how the other half of Cape Town live. Huts were erected with Galvanised metal and wood and anything else they could get their hands on. Inside the huts were makeshift beds tables and chairs. Materials of all sorts were used for bedclothes and curtains and outside an all-day fire served as cooker. Yet these people were smiling and welcoming. The children kicked a football made of rags on a clearing in the street that served as their football pitch. As the morning went on the women of the town made their way to the church, dressed impeccably in brightly coloured dresses and robes. We were welcomed to their church, where singing in unison was a joy to behold. They swayed and clapped, thanking God for what little they had and encouraged us to join in. It was an incredibly uplifting experience - well it was for me anyway. Some of the party saw it as an opportunity to squeeze out a few tears as the cameras rolled. Our trip to Cape Town was not complete without a trip to Robben Island, where Nelson Mandela was incarcerated for twenty-five years.

Disappointed that on my last trip ten years ago I never got out to it due to weather conditions, this for me was going to be a real highlight. On arrival in Cape Town three days ago what the whole party pause descended into Cape Town centre at about 1 o'clock and returned about 4:30 one of our party was asked what she did there. "I shopped for a while, got my hair done and oh popped over to Robben Island," she answered. Rumours had been circulating that the weather was too bad and the planned trip was not happening. She wasn't taking any chances. The security chief I had shared some beers with the night before informed me differently. "Strictly off the record Barry," he said, "make no mistake, tomorrow we go to Robben Island," and we did.

Because there were no trips the previous days there was a large queue of people there that morning. Our priority clearance meant that we only had to wait for forty minutes to an hour and then we were on the ferry I had promised myself I would someday be on.

The tour was fascinating. Mandela's cell, the exercise yard where they worked all day and the blazing sun chipping away at limestone rocks and even the place where they ate their meals were all shown to us by a former prison guard who for twenty years was in charge of Nelson Mandela. As the tour finished and we gathered for the return to Cape Town Head Producer Janine wondered what we made of it. Amid gasps of wonder and delight but having been able to see some recent history Collette, who is not controversial wondered why a former guard and not a former inmate would be a guide for this trip. The inmates she said would surely give a better insight into what really happened and that the guard was part of the regime that had put and kept Mandela there.

The silence was deafening, and disapproving glances were sent her way as to how she could criticise this man who have given us such a lovely tour and who was for the last ten years of his life, a great friend to the deceased Nelson Mandela, the fact that he could neither verify nor deny from the grave. My God, I thought the girl is getting political. Collette expressed exactly what I was thinking and obviously the producer Jannie was as well because they kept that piece in the show. Controversial or not, she had the last word. Back to the mainland we went in choppy seas. As we did, in front of us sat the member of the crew who had done a bit of shopping, got a hairdo and popped over to Robben island, all in the space of three and a half hours. Given that there had not been any ferries for the last three days I assumed she just swum it. As we spoke about the trip I could not resist a quick, "Sure you were there the other day" dig. Her friend sitting beside her looked at her oddly. A face that turned bright crimson, a dig in the ribs from Collette and an evil grin on my face, I fell silent. In the afternoon, it was down to the coast across the desolate plains to the Cape of Good Hope, where the two oceans meet, East meets west.

A beautiful part of the world with waves almost 15-feet tall crashing not a deserted beach. I was in heaven. On the way back we stopped to visit the Penguins at Boulder Beach. Cute looking Happy Feet creatures that would have your hand off in seconds. Then a final meal before boarding the bus back to the hotel.

We were leaving the next day but Francis had one more surprise. "Not quite finished yet!" he shouts, "tomorrow morning four of you are going shark fishing," and I was one of them. I'm delighted. Back to the sea again at 5am in the morning and Fisherman Finbarr is going too - an added bonus! I'm up at 4am, excited by the prospect of meeting Jaws face to face. We departed the hotel at 5am and two hours later were back on the coast. "Ship Ahoy," shouts Francis as we board our vessel and off we go into the middle of the ocean. Finbarr stands proudly up front, like Captain Blythe of Mutiny on the bounty, while Francis squeals like a Banshee every time some water spills onto the boat. I thought he was serious and went to comfort him. "Jesus Francis we are grand. Calm down," I said. He turned to me and smiled whispering, "television Barry, its good Television." Must be said it had worked on me. An hour later we heard a might cry of "Shark Coming Aboard, Shark coming aboard!" With that we all grabbed the rope to help pull this might aquatic beast in. One final pull and there he was, a tiny shark about four-feet long. "God," I exclaimed to Finbarr, "I was expecting Jaws!" "Aye," replied Finbarr. "Looks like we got Nemo. I've seen bigger cans of tuna." Two more sharks were pulled aboard, no bigger than the first one. They were baby sharks we were informed. Tagged and put back into the sea so that they could be tracked over periods of time we headed back towards land feeling a little under whelmed. Onto the minibus for the two-hour trip back to the hotel and we all fell asleep, even the film crew. We had gotten up at 5am to witness the capture of a great white shark and all we had gotten was Baby Shark. Back at the hotel we packed and got ready for our flight home - a fifteen-hour flight we reckoned. The cameras had stopped rolling. We were on the way to the Airport when Francis presents Collette with an Ostrich for her birthday which was that day. The stuffed toy was huge with long eyelashes and big lips. "It looks like you," he exclaimed before giving her a genuine hug. It was a wonderful way to finish. Finbarr and another lady from Limerick called Francis over. The ladies only purpose for the whole trip had been to be near Francis. She said she was eighty and her last wish was to go away with Francis and thankfully she got both her wish and the respect she deserved. Sixteen days of sometimes gruelling travelling and a lot of walking she got through and went home with a large smile on her face, and two very sore legs. As for my opinion, well I loved it. It really was my type of holiday. Loads of travelling and getting to see things I did not think I would ever have the chance to see. The production team were excellent and helped us in every way they could. They were professional but at the same time did not intimidate us in any way and showed us up in a good light.

As for the rest I will refer to Pat Stacey's column in the Evening Herald. After the first show came out the following July, as a regular reader of his column I read his views with interest, and by God Pat did not hold back. He slaughtered the show, referring to some participants as self-serving, attention-grabbing idiots. Who goes to South Africa on an obvious outdoor experience, while afraid of spiders and noises at night. He was scathing. By the way we did not escape his scorn. "Two dog groomers from Ashbourne, who seem to spend more time grooming themselves," he said and to be honest Pat was not far wrong and his article was completely right.

About four weeks after we got home and with the dust settled on our trip my mum was taken into hospital. It did not look good. As the daily reports said she remained stable, which meant no improvement, Collette contacted a girl on the production with whom we were very friendly, to see if Francis might give her a call. After two failed attempts to get through to mum and on this third effort Francis spoke to a senior nurse, explaining who he was and why he was calling. Things changed dramatically after that and within minutes a phone was brought to mum's bedside and Francis was on the other end.

"Now Mrs. Mc Donough" he said "This series with Barry and Collette is being shown on RTE in four weeks. I need you to get well quickly so that you can view properly!" Her recovery was remarkable after that and not only did she watch the show, but she also watched it in her own home. I will let you draw your own conclusions on that.

I have one outstanding memory of Francis Brennan that don't think I will ever forget. For the first week of the trip I never really conversed with Francis at all. Not that there were any problems between us - quite the opposite. In fact, we were very pleasant towards one another. There was just no connection between us - nothing in common. I guess as well as that most of the clique had him overwhelmed by the pedestal they had him sat on. After a visit one day to Nelson Mandela's statue in a park in Pretoria we descended a flight of steps to take us out of the park. It had just stopped raining. "Watch the steps," Francis cried, "they are very slippery." "Slippery when wet, eh Francis," I quipped. A Stoney silence ensued, disapproving stares at what was a very inappropriate comment, "Send him home," being written all over the cliques faces. "Not their best Album" said Francis. I turned in amazement as he said it. "No," he continued, "I much prefer their earlier stuff." "Yeah," I agreed. "Were you a fan," he asked regarding the New Jersey Rockers. "No," I said "I was more of a Ramones man," referring to the American Punk band of the 80's. "That's a pity," said Francis, "I'm more of a Clash man myself," he added to the stunned audience. A connection was made. Francis is well-loved throughout

Ireland. A pleasant, warm, and very affectionate man, he is also very astute. He spotted the rebellious streak in me and played his cards perfectly. He had me at the Clash. Sorry to say Francis, I'm still not a fan but if you ran for President of Ireland tomorrow you would have my vote and Collette's. Despite your very busy schedule you made time to make an old lady very happy. And I don't believe I have ever thanked you for that. Well I have now.

Chapter 29
A tale of Two Collies

Ger was on the phone. "Barry we are going to Australia for three and half weeks. Any chance of you minding Tara and Sammy." They were two smashing collies who we had groomed but never minded before. "When are you going" I asked. "Mid-December, back about the 9th of January." "Right Ger, let me have a look and see how we are fixed," I replied.

"Thanks," she said. "You know yourself that they are no trouble. A bit of food and attention and they will be fine." "Shouldn't be a problem," I said. "Do they come in early or late in the evening." "They don't come in at all," said Ger, "they sleep outside. Will not enter the house at all." "But Ger, December and January will be freezing." "Does not matter," she replied. "They won't come in- they just won't." With the outdoor area fully lit and two kennels on site, it would be a home from home for them. "I'll collect them on December 15th Ger," I said. "A weight off my mind Barry, thanks. No way am I putting those two in boarding kennels."

Tara and Sammy arrived. It took us about a day to work out how their sometimes-stormy relationship worked. First thing that morning I went to feed them, filling the bowls with a mixture of nuggets and meat and went to leave the area so they could dine in peace. Sammy went to his bowl and devoured it. Tara approached hers only to be met by a growling Sammy who instantly ate hers too. Tara retreated sheepishly. Crickey," I thought, "I need to rethink this." "It might be a one-off," suggested Collette, "what with the upset of being moved. Try again this evening."

I did and with the same result. Any time Tara approached her food Sammy growled and Tara fled, after which Sammy demolished her food. A simple solution - the gate to the outdoor area opened to the garden. So we simply let Tara out, kept Sammy in and she ate happily while he looked on in disgust. Once finished, Tara returned fully and happy and resumed sleeping. Sammy retreated sheepishly. The evenings were cold, but it never bothered either one a bit. A few showers came down but that did not phase either of them. Just after Christmas day the heavens opened. All day long it rained. Tara took to the kennel. A warm blanket and she was happy. Sammy remained outside. But eventually he went to join her. A combination of very wet and very wintry weather had forced him to seek refuge. He stuck his head into the kennel and Tara growled fiercely. Sammy tried again but to no avail. Tara was having none of it. She looked Sammy in the eye and basically told him to shift.

Sammy gave up and despondently went to the other kennel and went inside. You knew by his face that he was not happy and wanted a cuddle. These scenes played out over the next three days. Tara ate in the garden and no cosying up for Sammy. And yet if you parted the two of them they would cry incessantly until reunited. Rain, wind or snow, nothing deterred them. All they wanted was fed and a little attention. Well, that is all Tara wanted. Sammy sometimes played outside with Impala but never for very long. He just wanted to get back to his soul mate Tara. These were two old school Collies. Tough, resilient, and adverse to any weather conditions they also showed us great affectation and it was very easy to give it back to the two beautiful dogs like them.

When Ger came home and I brought them back, the two dogs bounded out of the van and ran straight to their kennel. Tara in first and Sammy in after her. He was accepted without any problem. I mentioned to Ger about her blanking Sammy and Ger looked surprised.

"Good Barry I have never seen that," she said. "Well," I said "for three and a half weeks that how it was. He would not let her eat so she kicked him out of the bed and now the two of them are in there getting on like a house on fire like nothing ever happened."

"Well," said Ger laughing, "maybe with the kennels Tara just wanted value for money." I laughed, not really believing it but as I drove out the gate there were two smiling heads looking out of the kennel at me. I thought to myself, "Maybe, just Maybe."

Chapter 30
Georgy and the unappreciated favour

"Can you do me a favour," the next-door neighbour Marc enquired. "Of course," I replied to Marc, a man who had done several favours for me in the past. "We are getting a dog," he announced. "Oh Good," says I. "Saying that we must go to England for a while and she has to be collected on a certain date - the 28th in Portlaoise. "No problem," I said "I can do that no problem." Collette came with me so the dog could come home in her lap.

We went down to Portlaoise on the morning of the 28th and duly collected the beautiful Shit Zu pup. Cuddled up on Collette lap, we brought her home, gave her a quick wash and blow dry and she curled up in a bed in the living room. She slept soundly that night and the next morning loped about happily, waiting for her new family, when they eventually came back from England.

Marc came in with his two overly excited girls to collect their new baby. She's gorgeous, exclaimed Marc. Annette and the girls are in heaven. We are going to name her Georgy. About ten weeks later Annette asked if we would give her a little trim. "Of course," I said, "I will collect her in the morning."

At 9am the next morning I knocked on their door to collect Georgy. His cute little head peeped out the window, then she went ballistic, barking and trying to find somewhere to hide.

Annette arrived at the front door with Georgy in her arms squiring to escape and looking up at her as if to say, "Don't hand me to him." Georgy obviously remembered the last time she saw me when I drove her away from her loving family, kept her prisoner for two nights and then handed her over to someone new. And now she thought I was going to do it again. Georgy had me down as a dog trafficker.

30 seconds later Georgy was in Collette's hands in the salon. A dream to groom, loves a wash and quite content in her drying cage, not a woof out of her for two and a half hours. As I lifted her to bring her back next-door Georgy was meek as a lamb. "Look at that," said Collette "She's gotten over it now."

Not a bit of it. As soon as I got her next door she jumped out of my arms, turned, and started to bark wildly again, before scuttling off to hide under the couch. "What was she like?" Annette enquired. "Well, for the past two hours or so not a bark, a pleasure to groom. As soon as she gets home? well obviously it is me she doesn't trust," I said. Annette laughed. "Not to worry Barry she will in time."

But she did not. Five years on and it's still the same story. When I knock on the door off she goes, racing around and barking loudly. Seconds later the quietest dog in the world for the next few hours and then home again and she kicks off. The sight of me going to the van in the morning is enough to set Georgy off. Or when she is outside her front door and spots me coming, she bolts indoors and hides.

In the Salon Georgy never lets out as much as a whimper. She has even stayed over for three nights when the family are away and not a peep out of her. Collette reckons she thinks that so long as she keeps quiet she has a good chance of getting home alive. I just do not think Georgy will ever forgive me for kidnapping her from her family and bringing her up the country before joining the family she obviously adores.

I reckon that she thinks that this evil man is very capable of doing it again. And he is not to be trusted. They say elephants never forget. Georgy never will.

Our own personal Jar of Hearts

Hey Ma, it's the Doggy Man!

Epilogue

So there you have it. Thirty years of farming followed by sixteen years of dog grooming means that I have spent all my adult life in the company of animals. People often ask me do I prefer the farming or the dogs. For me that's an easy one to answer.

Farming is a tough grind and a lonely one. The hours are long and you might not see another person for a week. Collecting dogs means interacting with people all the time. It creates so many funny situations, many of which I have shared in this book with you. For me, these experiences have been priceless. I wouldn't change my job for the world.